I0037350

90 DAYS *to* YOUR FIRST REAL ESTATE INVESTMENT PURCHASE

The **Essential Daily Action Guide** to Profiting in Residential Real Estate Investing Like A Pro, Even If You Never Purchased A Property and Are on a Shoe-String Budget

ROBERT GILL JR.

TEACHINGPRESS

Copyright © 2020 Teaching Press

No part of this publication may be reproduced, stored in a retrieval system or transmitted in any form or by any means electronic, mechanical, photocopying, recording, scanning or otherwise. Except as permitted under Sections 107 or 108 of the 1976 United States Copyright Act, without the prior written permission of the Publisher. Requests to the Publisher for permissions should be addressed to: Teaching Press, Suite 1, Summit, New Jersey 07901.

Limit of Liability/Disclaimer of Warranty: The Publisher and the author make no representations or warranties with respect to the accuracy or completeness of the contents of this work and specifically disclaim all warranties, including without limitation warranties of fitness for a particular purpose. No warranty may be created or extended by sales or promotional materials. The advice and strategies contained herein may not be suitable for every situation. This work is sold with the understanding that the publisher is not engaged in rendering medical, legal or other professional advice or services. If professional assistance is required, the services of a competent professional person should be sought. Neither the Publisher nor the author shall be liable for damages arising here from. The fact that an individual, organization or website is referred to in this work as a citation and/or potential source of further information does not mean that the author or the Publisher endorses the information that the individual, organization or website may provide or recommendations they or it may make. Further, readers should be aware that Internet websites listed in this work may have changed or disappeared between when this work was written and when it is read.

For general information on our other products and services or to obtain technical support, please contact our Customer Service at (908) 273-5600.

Teaching Press publishes its books in a variety of electronic and print formats. Some content that appears in print may not be available in electronic books and vice versa.

TRADEMARKS: Teaching Press is a registered trademark of Teaching Press and may not be used without written permission. All other trademarks are the property of their respective owners.

ISBN: Print 978-0-5787-1827-9

Interior Design by FormattedBooks.com

DEDICATION

To my wonderful wife.
It is a privilege to share my business, life, and love with you. I appreciate all your support, encouragement, and hard work, which have been a never-ending source of inspiration and pride to me.

CONTENTS

The 90-Day Investor's Checklist
(<u>Never</u> leave home without this…)

INVESTMENT ANALYSIS CHECKLIST

This checklist includes:

- ❖ The 1% Rule for Property Cash Flow Valuation
- ❖ The 55% Rule for Net Operating Income (NOI) Valuation
- ❖ Income and Expenses Found for Most Investment Properties

The last thing we want is for you to miss your 90-day goal because you were not prepared.

To receive your real estate investment checklist, visit the link:

www.teachingpress.com

INTRODUCTION

YOUR EXCITING JOURNEY BEGINS HERE!

"Ninety percent of all millionaires become so through owning real estate. More money has been made in real estate than in all industrial investments combined. The wise young [person] or wage earner of today invests [their] money in real estate."
—Andrew Carnegie

I f I asked you how to become a millionaire, chances are you would say, "Buy a winning lottery ticket" or, "Wait to inherit from a rich relative." None of these are likely to happen, though. There is a much more predictable way you can build wealth. Begin by investing in real estate, and then, with some work, the goal of a million dollars or more of net worth is certain—all without chance.

All in all, it took me forty-two years to become a real estate millionaire. But it only took me nine years from the day I bought my first investment property. If someone had mentored me earlier in life, teaching me simple investing steps, I probably would have become a real estate millionaire far sooner. Those who will follow these careful instructions will have built significant wealth while most of their peers are still struggling.

In life, no one gets something for nothing, and that is just as true in building real estate wealth. Wealth building does not happen without work; it involves some self-discipline and even some temporary sacrifice. But by slowly purchasing and renting out the homes, you can bring your net worth to the one-million-dollar mark within ten to fifteen years. You can continue to get rich in real estate, while everyone else you knew at age twenty-five continues with little to nothing in the bank.

Most of you may not have even started saving for retirement. Some might admit to having little savings for a rainy day. That can be financially embarrassing. It does not have to be that way, as it can change if you know how to do it. This book is your secret.

You might not think you need to read this book today. However, if you do not, you will be unnecessarily delaying your first important decision—to change your finances for the better. If you put it off, you will be unnecessarily delaying the all-important opportunity for monthly cash flow and the growth of your net worth. Did you realize that once you make your first investment, your wealth starts to grow even while you sleep, not to mention the pride and joy of accomplishment with ownership?

This book will give you the best techniques for building a passive income through rental real estate. By following the instructions, you will find profitable real estate deals that will give you an excellent return on your investment year after year. This first investment will provide you with a great source of cash flow and steady increases in your net worth into your early retirement and for the rest of your life.

What you will learn here will change your life and provide you the independence that most of us crave. If real estate investing is what you want to do, then by following these chapters you can employ the eight major steps to your first real estate investment.

We have organized the book for you to purchase an investment property in 90-days and become a real estate investor. It will change your life.

The first step starts here in the introduction. To educate you on real estate investment techniques—what to look for, how to find good deals, and how to overcome the competition.

You will then practice property analysis using a rule of thumb, as described in Chapter 6. We show you how to practice property analysis until you are an expert at it. The more you practice, the better the deals you will find. Please make sure you memorize the *one-percent rule* we show you, so you do not waste your time on bad deals.

As you become confident in your analytics, you can begin your searches by looking for deals online. You can use Internet sites such as realtor.com, zillow.com, redfin.com, loopnet.com, rentometer.com, and your local multiple listing (MLS) sites.

Once you are familiar with these listing sites, you will find a local real estate agent specializing in investment properties. You will have the broker set you up with automatic email listings on the property types you are searching for as soon as they list for sale.

The next step is to ask your newfound broker-teammate to recommend local lenders. You will ask these lenders to provide financial preapproval letters to use in making offers.

With those steps in place, you will begin the habit of analyzing at least one real deal every day. We show you how this is accomplished, and you will get to enjoy it.

Your goal is to make at least one offer each week. Of course, as you gain experience, you can make your offers more often. More offers equal more opportunities.

Like a closed loop in your automatic investment routine, you will repeat these last several steps until you have closed on your first buy.

Yes, this is work, and we admit that. It is the most efficient and quickest protocol you can use to become successful in real estate investment in a short period.

There is a second challenge, it may be the biggest challenge. That of finding good deals. Most new investors struggle to find them. We will explain all about completing successful searches to keep you ahead of the competition and make you a great investor.

We will show you how to do it with little or no money down if you are just starting on a small budget.

By following these techniques and the information we provide you in these chapters, you can become a first-time investor in 90-days, or less.

If you have decided that it is time to invest in real estate, this book will be your best friend.

Please turn the page to begin your journey, as now is the time to start on your first day as an official real estate investor.

CHAPTER ONE

LET'S START

"Now, one thing I tell everyone is learn about real estate. Repeat after me: real estate provides the highest returns, the greatest values and the least risk."
— Armstrong Williams, entrepreneur

OVERCOMING YOUR FEARS

The fear of starting something new is an evolutionary trait. We all experience it. It may be a human weakness, yet it is the most common feeling we internalize when beginning something new. Often, that great weakness can be trained to be your greatest strength. A story worth repeating is of a caring father of a young boy who decided to enroll his son in a martial arts class to rebuild his confidence after the boy lost his left arm in a freak camping accident.

The father hired an experienced Japanese martial arts master to teach the boy. With his wise instruction, the boy became skillful after several months. The boy could not understand why during all this time he was taught only one move.

"Master," the frustrated boy asked, "Shouldn't you be teaching me more moves?"

"My young student, this move may be the only one you know, but it is the only one you will ever need to know," answered the master.

The young boy strongly believed in his master, and so he continued his martial arts practice.

Some months later, his teacher announced the boy was ready to compete. The boy easily won the first two fights, much to his delight. But the third match was challenging. Then, as the competition wore on, his opponent gave him an opening, which the boy used to win his third match. Shocked, the boy realized he was now in the finals.

This time it would not be an easy win. It appeared the boy was mismatched in that his opponent outweighed him and was stronger and far more experienced. As the match got underway, the referee was so concerned about the safety of the young boy that he stopped the match.

"No, no," the master intervened, "Let the match continue."

Shortly after the match resumed, the boy's opponent dropped his guard. At once, the boy pounced using the practiced move to win the match. He received the competition trophy for his class.

On the drive home, the boy asked, "Master, how is it that I won the tournament with just a single move?"

The master replied, "You won because you have mastered one of the most difficult moves in all the martial arts. The only defense for that move is for your opponent to grip your left arm."

The lesson here is that with the right training and practice, almost any weakness can be overcome, and impossible feats are performed. I know from my experience that I could not move forward in real estate investing until I overcame my weakness, which was my fear of investing in real estate. How does one move forward under those circumstances? I think you will agree the answer is simple: our motivation must overcome our defeatist feelings. If we can learn to develop motivation, we can succeed in great accomplishments in life.

SETTING UP GOALS TO SUCCEED

Goals are what give us motivation in life. They show a sense of direction. It is what allows our minds to focus on a target. When we have a specific endpoint in mind, we automatically avoid certain distractions and stay focused on the goal. Goals are the tools to focus our energy. Setting goals for us is a way to fuel ambition. A goal is like having a map to give us direction.

Many of us have giant dreams that seem impossible to carry out. It is easy to feel discouraged when you are staring at a massive, seemingly insurmountable mountain. Research has proven that achieving smaller milestones provides real motivation and greater contentment.

This book sets up a big goal—ninety days to your first real estate investment. Achieving such a laudable goal will provide you with benefits way beyond a real estate asset. It will melt away fears, provide you with extraordinary self-confidence and self-worth, and put you on a path of independence.

It is a big goal, we agree. But this book takes you step-by-step and teaches you what to do. We have set your goal to purchase within three months after you finish the book. The deadline is tight, so you will miss the target if you slack off. It is well worth the work that you put into it. So here we start down the investment road. As you take on the challenge, you will be distracted with obstacles and disappointments along the way. The road is not a smooth one. As they say, if it were so easy, everyone would be doing it. It is not easy, but it is incredibly worthwhile.

Each chapter takes you through the steps of helping you find your first investment property. Why would that motivate you?

To answer that question accurately needs you to think long-term, as real estate investing is a get-rich-slow proposition. With this well-thought-out ninety-day investment plan, you will soon be able to leave the nine-to-five grind and retire at a young age. Because the critical part of real estate investment is that you can use what income you have available now, including your salary, to buy your property investments using debt. This method, called leverage, allows you to invest more significant amounts without using your own money.

Investing is perhaps the most essential piece of your financial future—but often, it takes a while before we understand this truth. Some of you get that now, but you still have not put it into action. Examine why that may be and what you can do about it.

LACK OF INVESTMENT

Unfortunately, in our day and age, even minor investing is avoided. As an example, fifty-two percent of Americans are avoiding the stock market—either by not buying stocks or mutual funds or investing in retirement accounts such as a 401(k) or an IRA. Among the non-investors surveyed, fifty-three percent said they do not have the money to invest, and twenty-one percent said they do not trust stockbrokers or financial advisers.[1]

Leading to the conclusion that so many of us are not financially prepared for retirement. Then we learn of those making promises, promises, promises. A study by the financial services firm Edward Jones found that ninety percent of respondents ages 18 to 35 say they either have started saving for retirement or plan to start before turning thirty. Just seven percent of that group plan to start saving for retirement in their 40s. Meanwhile, when looking at respondents ages 35 to 44, only sixty-four percent began saving in their 30s or earlier.[2]

Americans Believe Real Estate is the
BEST LONG-TERM INVESTMENT

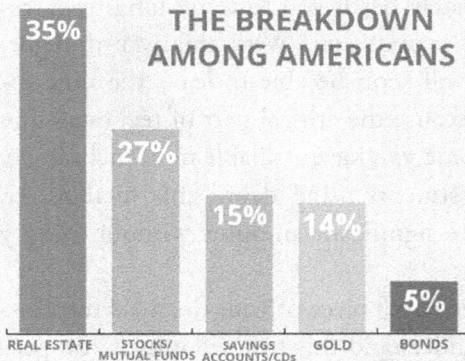

THE BREAKDOWN AMONG AMERICANS

35% — REAL ESTATE
27% — STOCKS/MUTUAL FUNDS
15% — SAVINGS ACCOUNTS/CDs
14% — GOLD
5% — BONDS

MAY 2019 Gallup Poll Results

Stocks have had a strong 2019, with the major U.S. stock indices establishing or nearing record highs in April and early May. Still, more Americans continue to believe real estate (35%) is a superior long-term investment to stocks (27%) or other investment options.
- Gallup

Source: https://news.gallup.com/poll/251696/real-estate-leads-stocks-best-investment.aspx

Figure 1. According to a May 2019 Gallup poll, Americans still regard real estate as a better bet for long-term investment. Gallup found that Americans who own both stocks and a home are also divided as to which is the best investment, with 40% choosing real estate

With those results in mind, according to a 2018 survey by GO Banking Rates, nearly half of Americans are at risk of retiring broke. It found that forty-two percent have less than $10,000 saved for retirement. Another report from the Economic Policy Institute (EPI), using 2013 data, found that many Americans are unprepared for retirement.[3]

That is just the bad news on retirement. But what about saving for college? Out of ten families surveyed, nine said they knew their student would attend college as early as his or her enrollment in preschool. Despite that knowledge, far fewer families—less than 4 in 10—had created a plan to pay for all years of college before their child enrolled.[4]

According to Sallie Mae, forty-two percent of families went into debt in 2017 to cover some college expenses. The thinking of families who borrow to pay for college is different from that of those who do not borrow in several ways. Those who borrowed were not likely to have a plan to pay for college, and they were not confident they made the right financial decisions about how they are paying for college.[5]

Princeton Survey Research Associates found that twenty-one percent of working Americans in 2017 is not saving any part of their income, which remains unchanged from the answer consumers gave the survey in 2016. Just 25 percent are saving more than 10 percent of their incomes, down from 28 percent in 2016.[6]

What are the primary reasons Americans are not saving more money? The No. 1 answer: Thirty-eight percent said their expenses were excessive. Expenses may not be under their control, given that wages have remained stagnant in recent years. Some 16.4 percent of those surveyed replied that they "hadn't gotten around to it." The third and fourth reasons? Just over 16 percent said they did not have a good enough job, and 13 percent said they were struggling under debt.

FEAR OF INVESTMENT

Sixty-five percent of adults say they find stock investing to be frightening or intimidating, according to October 23, 2018, Ally Financial survey.[7]

Such lack of action credited to fear of loss. Behavioral economists have a name for this normal psychological dislike. They call it *loss aversion*. "People naturally have this fear of losing money, and its effects what would otherwise be rational judgment," says Robert Koppel, author of *Investing and the Irrational Mind.*[8]

Investing can be a bit scary. You will have to learn to cope with this psychological issues if you want to learn to invest. Mastering one's emotions while investing is a healthy challenge, but all successful investors have done this.

This fear is misplaced, and it is. We should be more worried about reaching retirement age and not having enough.

Those that fear investing need to reorient the way they look at it. Instead of thinking about investing, think about protecting. Look at investing in the way it is designed—not as a get-rich scheme, but to protect what you have earned and to increase those assets over time. Investing equates to keeping your savings safe and growing so you can pay for college and vacations and retire in comfort.

Most of us think of the stock market when the term *investment* comes up. Under the right circumstances, real estate offers an alternative that can be lower risk, yield better returns, and provide the most significant opportunity for diversification. More people invest in the stock market, perhaps because it does not take as much time or money to buy stock.

However, when you buy a real estate investment, you gain a piece of land or property. It takes more time to research compared to an investment in stock. But unlike stocks, you make money several ways. First, money comes to you from the monthly rent. You gain through property appreciation. Your mortgage loan is paid down every month out of the rent collections, giving you added net worth even as you sleep. Your real estate can be leveraged to make it possible to expand your holdings even if you cannot afford to pay cash outright. Investors can also take advantage of large tax benefits.

Buying investment real estate often needs more capital than investing in stocks and mutual funds. When buying property, investors have more leverage over their money, enabling them to buy a more valuable investment.

That is why millionaires say that real estate is still the best investment you can make today. The question is, how to begin? Admittedly, getting started as a real estate investor can be challenging, especially if you have little money to start. I think that it might surprise you how far you can go with as little as $10,000.

I have bought and sold all types of investment properties: single-family, multi-family, garden apartments, strip malls, and office buildings as well as land. We have made these buys from sellers using real estate brokers, through foreclosures, and through tax-free 1031 exchanges where we traded a garden apartment for two office buildings. At their height, our real estate assets totaled over twenty-million dollars, with twelve million in equity.

BENEFITS OF INVESTING

There are so many benefits to investing that it is something everyone should take part in. Getting started is easy, and it makes little sense not to. The purpose of investing should appeal to everyone, as it builds wealth and provides long-term financial stability.

Investing is not savings. Investing is for growth. With saving, there has been almost no return these past few years and, as a result, this it offers little growth. You might remember years ago when the average CD yields exceeded ten percent. Those days are over and long gone. You will not find returns anywhere close to that now. The average one-year CD returned just 0.45 percent APY in 2020, according to a Bankrate survey. Between 2019 and 2020, the inflation rate was 2.05 percent, meaning your CD would be losing 1.6 percent of its value in the bank each year (2.05 – 0.45). It is the opposite of growth – it is a loss.

You can probably see from this real-life example that if you do not invest and grow your money, thanks to inflation, you will lose money over time.

Inflation is the general increase in prices that happens throughout the year. It reduces the buying power of your money. The rate of inflation can vary; though today it is 2.05 percent, historically inflation has averaged around three percent.

If, instead, you invest your money, say, in the stock market, you can expect a much higher return. Historically, the stock market has returned an average of ten percent yearly before inflation. Of course, stock market returns vary significantly from year to year. There are no guarantees in the market, but this ten percent average has held remarkably steady for a long time. If you make such a decision, you will grow your investment and stay ahead of inflation.

Investing is how wealth builds. There are many ways to invest and grow your money. If you want to build your wealth, you need to create an investment plan based on your goals.

Investing allows your money to work for you so you can make your retirement goals and live comfortably. Investing enables compound interest. This is what happens when your interest starts earning on interest.

Another extraordinary benefit of investing is saving on taxes. If you set up a retirement account such as a 401(k), IRA, or SEP, you avoid paying taxes on the amounts you deposit each year. You pay taxes when you withdraw the funds, at which point you should be in a lower tax bracket.

Warren Buffet has this advice: "Never depend on a single income; invest in creating a second source."[9]

You can summarize this into a simple premise, namely, that if you don't invest now and continue not to, you will be rudely awakened sometime in the future, realizing that retirement is not a choice for you.

CELEBRITY INVESTORS

Perhaps you cannot act, but you can invest and reap the same rewards that many Hollywood celebrities have been seeing. Hollywood types have set aside their fears of investing in real estate and have learned that it is easy to make their money work for them.

Ellen DeGeneres is the Hollywood investment queen. She has closed $150 million in real estate deals in just two years. DeGeneres has bought and sold at least eight homes in Carpinteria, Beverly Hills, Montecito, Carpinteria, and elsewhere.

In *Home*, her book about her real estate and decorating adventures, DeGeneres wrote that she had bought and renovated nearly a dozen homes over the past twenty-five years. When she was 13, she thought she would be an interior designer.

We do not want to leave out singer and songwriter Taylor Swift, with her $81 million of mansions and penthouses. She has yet to do as well as DeGeneres but is catching up. She has benefited extraordinarily by buying high-end rental properties that are gaining value and that provides her added cash flow while she continues to tour, write, and record. "For others, such as former *Baywatch* and *Melrose Place* actor David Charvet, they were astute enough to realize that a beau-hunky TV actor often has a specific shelf life and looked to real estate investment as a second act."[10]

Other Hollywood real estate investors are also well-known celebrities: Jeremy Renner, Jennifer Aniston, Diane Keaton, Arnold Schwarzenegger, Vanilla Ice, Brad Blumenthal, and Ashton Kutcher, to name a few more.

What do these actor types know that you may not? Real estate investing pays, and it pays big time.

OVERCOMING THE FEAR OF INVESTMENT

Overcoming the fear of investment begins through reading and educating yourself about the types of investments available to you and how they might respond to your long-term goals. Then you must take the plunge and invest. The best place to start is with a 401K retirement fund. You might also wish to put a little money in a mutual fund to get the feel of the market's ups and downs. Your first-time investing should only be with little capital. Seek out advice from someone you trust who has the experience, or a knowledgeable family member.

Ignore the ups and downs that are the regular part of the stock market. Base successful investing in sticking with a long view of the market. Investopedia reports that in the past 90 years, the average annual return of the S&P 500 has been around ten percent.[10]

OVERCOMING THE FEAR OF REAL ESTATE INVESTING

Real estate investing is alive and thriving in every state of the union. You hear about it in the office, on television, and maybe at your club. You may even own a house, and indeed, your parents may. What about that cousin of yours who brags about his rental properties? In other words, real estate investing is all around you. You are missing out.

What is holding you back? We covered it before. Your reluctance, about this real estate investing, is held up by an undefined fear that we should explore.

Overcoming any problem begins with understanding the cause. What are the fears preventing you from making financial decisions you have to make?

What are Those Fears?

Fear can immobilize us. They can prevent us from realizing our goals and dreams and explain our lack of investment progress. These fears can cause us to lose hope and think less of ourselves. They are a great life negative.

Realize that investing is not a matter of life-and-death. The primary fear in investing is the fear of failing. In life, we fall off the horse sometimes. We get back up, dust ourselves off, and ride on. That is the story of life. Nothing is perfect. The real failure is not getting back on the horse. Fearing the horse will immobilize you, but you are stronger and smarter than that.

What is the answer? It is to reveal the facts and actions to take in an investment plan. You write down your goals and, in bullet points, the measures you will take to get you there. A written plan reduces your chances of failure while increasing your success.

Of course, you will not be putting a million dollars in the bank with your first investment. Because it is your first deal and you are still learning, you may not create as much cash flow as you calculated. This is the deal to cut your teeth on and to walk away with a significant amount of experience. You will have broken through the fear barrier and gained immeasurable confidence you can use to find the next deal.

Overcome Investment Fear with Knowledge

If one of your fears of investing is the lack of funds, then there is great news for you. You do not need much money. You can start with a budget of as little as $10,000. If you do not have that amount, now that you are focused and have the want, saving up should not take too long. Say you put away $500 a month. If you started from zero, in twenty months, you would hit your goal. Meanwhile, you will not waste your time if you begin following the advice in this book and start looking for and analyzing deals for practice.

Let us, for a moment, move away from the topic of fear of real estate investing. Instead, we can lessen the entire subject to a fear of decision-making. After all, it amounts to a yes or no action plan to make your first investment. That is the decision that you must make. It does not need to be fearful. Instead, what it needs is education. It wants to research the benefits to see that they outweigh any disadvantages. All successful business decisions go through the same process, known as a *cost-benefit analysis*.

Business uses a decision-making method known as a cost-benefit analysis to analyze decisions. This is a method to discover the merits of a business idea. In this case, the choice is whether to invest in real estate or not. In practice, the analyst lists all the benefits of taking a specific action, then subtracts all the costs associated with making such a move. It can be more sophisticated, as some analysts build models to assign a dollar value to intangible items such as the benefits and costs associated with living in a town. But we do not need to go that far.

Proper decision-making is about developing a list of wants. Then you look for opportunities meeting most or all those needs. For example, if you are thinking about buying a new car, you will consider several features—mileage, horsepower, and similar factors. If you are deciding to invest in a CD, you will compare banks and interest rates.

As an example, when a CD of ours came due recently, instead of automatically renewing it, we shopped around and found in these times of minuscule interest rates a local bank providing three times the interest rate as the old CD in a new savings account. So, we opened an account at the new bank and made the deposit there. This cost-benefit analysis we made was a simple one and cannot be compared to that of a real estate investment. But the process is the same.

Let us work through a theoretical cost-benefit analysis of a potential real estate rental investment. Most people cannot answer the question of comparing real estate to the stock market. If they try to, it is often with a skewed apples-to-oranges comparison such as a 3-percent real estate appreciation versus a 6-percent average stock return over time. If you hear this, rest assured, the person has no idea about real estate investment returns. Let us look at two examples:

Long-term buy and hold stock investment:

Assume you invest $10,000 into an S&P index fund and leave it untouched for 30 years. With an average annual return, your account would be valued at $76,122.11. If you decide to cash in, you will be obligated to pay a 15-percent capital gains tax, so you will receive $64,704.17.

Long-term buy and hold rental investment:

With that same $10,000, you buy a $40,000 rental property. You borrow $30,000 at a 4-percent interest rate for a thirty-year term. True to form, as with most real estate, your property appreciates at an average of 4 ¼ percent a year. Your monthly rents are $200, which nets you $40.00 a month in cash flow.

Appreciation. By growing four and a quarter percent yearly, after 30 years the property is worth $139,425. That is more than the original purchase price of $40,000, the property has appreciated by $99,425 ($139,425 minus $40,000).

Equity Growth. You began your investment with a $40,000 property purchase using $10,000 of equity to buy it. Over 30 years, the income from your rents paid off the entire loan. You have increased your equity by $30,000 ($40,000 – $10,000).

Rental Income. After maintenance and capital costs, vacancies, and property management costs, your net before-tax cash flow is $480 yearly. However, because of depreciation write-off, the cash flow is not taxed. If we can assume an average rent increase of two percent a year, net rental income will total $22,523.00 over 30 years.

Total Return:	
Appreciation	$99,425
Equity Growth	$30,000
Rental Income	$22,523
Total Earnings	$151,948

Earnings, before you pay any tax on a sale, are $151,948, more than double the $76,122 that would have been earned on the stock investment.

CHOICES FOR THE FUTURE

When the property mortgage is paid off you have several future choices:

- You can pay the capital gains and depreciation recapture tax and sell.
- You can delay paying any taxes through a 1031 real estate exchange.
- You can simply decide to hold on to the property and continue collecting a larger amount of rental income.
- You can get a reverse mortgage to supplement your retirement.
- You can borrow against the property, buy that yacht you have always dreamed about, and have your tenants pay it off as they did the mortgage.

It is impossible to make an equal comparison between a securities investment and a real estate investment. Real estate offers different kinds of benefits beyond straight appreciation. Both types of investing have advantages, with real estate offering several benefits unavailable in stock investing.

Now that you have compared the two choices of putting your money in stock and putting your money into investment real estate, note that these are not limiting choices. They are not limited to either-or, as you can invest in both simultaneously. However, if you could only choose one, which would it be? We have prepared five excellent reasons the real estate rental investment is the better choice:

A wide number of real estate investment choices. As you will see in later chapters, there are many real estate investment choices available to you. These choices include raw land, house, duplexes, commercial properties, wholesaling, and flipping to name a few. Moving up, you can choose to invest in commercial properties such as strip malls, office buildings, and warehouse-type properties. You also have many investment choices to invest in alone or in partnership with another investor.

Real estate is a physical asset. While securities are represented on paper documents you will rarely see, real estate can be visited and inspected as it is a hard asset. Unlike stocks with risks that allow their value to fall to zero, real estate increases in value over time because of a demand for housing, office, and retail space.

Less volatility owning real estate. It is given that stock tends to be highly volatile. Its value rises and falls up and down after it is purchased. Stocks are also dependent on market, news, and demand.

Real estate does not reveal itself in this way. Its value remains stable increasing by inflation. Thus, it is considered a safer investment.

Real estate provides more control. Real estate gives you control over how it is managed. You can manage it yourself or use a management company. You can find the tenant, set the rent rate, and keep the property to your standards.

Great tax advantages. Real estate investment comes with excellent tax advantages. You can take off all your expenses, including interest on your mortgage. You can also shelter your real estate income using the depreciation the tax code allows.

So far you have learned about all the benefits available to a real estate investor. Here we want to address the fears of investing a second time to summarize what we have presented here.

Actions to Take to Overcome Real Estate Investment Fears

- Educate yourself: Read books on real estate investment. Watch YouTube videos. Listen to real estate vlogs
- Perform financial analysis on real estate investment properties until you become comfortable doing it
- Join a local real estate investment club
- Put limits on your capital investment
- Use other people's money by controlling instead of owning.
- Wait to launch

There are two primary reasons those who believe in real estate investing have not taken part. They are a lack of money and various apprehensions leading to a fear of investing. Both resolved through action.

TO REMOVE FEAR, YOU MUST FIRST EMBRACE IT

Noam Shpancer Ph.D. writes in Psychology Today, "… avoiding anxiety maintains and magnifies it. To get rid of your anxiety, you should capitalize on the principle of habituation using 'exposure.' Exposure is by far the most potent medicine known to psychology. It is responsible, or indirectly responsible, for most improvement in therapy—any therapy, but particularly the treatment of anxiety. Exposure entails facing your fears, which makes it aversive in the short-term. But many worthy long-term goals involve short-term discomfort."[11]

In other words, recognize the anxiety for what it is, embrace it, then "pull the trigger," go out, and as uncomfortable as it might seem at first, just do it—invest.

ACTION REINFORCES DOING, DOING REINFORCES HABITUATION

A common form of learning is through habituation. Habituation is something that happens regularly in your everyday life, yet you are largely unaware of it. The most significant reason in your future financial well-being is simply getting started in investing. The act of doing so will reinforce the habit, lessen anxiety, and reinforce getting rich slowly. The way forward is through building your knowledge and developing a savings discipline.

Knowledge. The more you study a subject, the more you learn it. The more you master it, the more you will understand and be comfortable with it. This applies to learning to drive, skiing, playing an instrument, and of course, investing. The more you learn about a subject, the less intimidating it becomes. It will lessen the inclination for making rookie mistakes and build your confidence to stay with it in the long run.

Set investment money aside. Success begins with making lifestyle changes such as simplifying our lives and lessening extraneous expenses. It can be as simple an act as packing lunch instead of buying lunch. Put the daily savings in a jar and bank it once a month. Focus on what you can save. That simple act will return dividends as you build investment capital and make rental property purchases in the coming years. Decide to build the future for you and your family by saving.

SUMMARY

If you remember our story at the beginning of this chapter, you should remember the missing arm. The young man overcame that weakness through training by doing. He wanted to know more, but his teacher had him focus on only one move, one objective, and then he studied it until he mastered it. Perhaps you will give me a license to equate that weakness to that of beginning investors filled with apprehension and concern that they may lack the capital to begin an investment program. This book is all the training you need to overcome those weaknesses and, in ninety days or less, enter the competition—which is to put into action all you learned and earn that winning trophy—your first investment property. Let us do this together.

NEXT STEPS

In the next chapter, we look at the variety of real estate investments that are designed for a beginner. We examine the pros and cons of each. By the end of the chapter, you should have a firm idea of the specific property type best suited to you. It should be an exciting chapter as we explore the benefits of a variety investment types. Even if you know in advance what class of property you want to specialize in, you will learn a great deal about alternatives. The next step is to read the chapter and decide on the property you want to embrace.

CHAPTER TWO

THE PROS AND CONS OF REAL ESTATE INVESTMENT

"Real estate investing, even on a very small scale, remains a tried and true means of building an individual's cash flow and wealth."

—Robert Kiyosaki

The multimillionaire and oil tycoon J. Paul Getty was once asked by a magazine for a short article explaining his success. The publication enclosed a check for three hundred and sixty dollars. In reply, Getty wrote: "Some people find oil. Others don't."

We promise that unlike Getty, we will explain all the steps you need to take to build your real estate investment portfolio to build wealth. As described in our last chapter, there are many reasons you should get over your hesitancy and begin your real estate investment plans now.

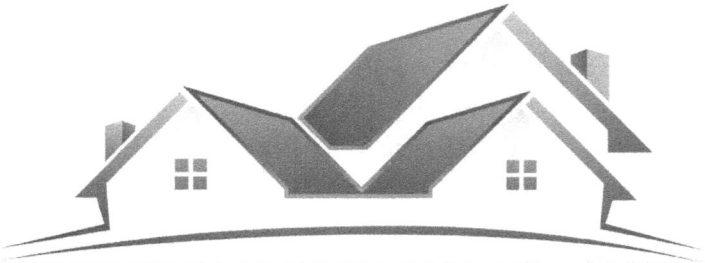

WHY YOU SHOULD CHOOSE REAL ESTATE TO INVEST IN

The **US tax code** is written around real estate. It provides the best tax benefits of any investment in this country. It many instances it will totally shelter your **income**.

You will enjoy real estate investing and owning tangible property in **America, the greatest country in the world.** With careful investing anyone can get **rich in real estate investment.**

Once you **overcome your fear of investing** increasing your real estate portfolio over time will make you **feel joyful.**

Investment real estate produce **passive income** can earn that income even as you sleep

You can start in real estate investing at **any time and at any age.** You will not get rich quickly. It will take **five to ten years** to realize the cash flow and appreciate you are aiming for.

The approach to investment is **knowledge.** The next step is **read this book to learn** about real estate investment and how to **make your first investment.**

Figure 2. Why you should choose real estate to invest in.

If you are looking to grow your net worth, while making passive monthly income, look no further than real estate investment.

If you are still hesitant about becoming a real estate investor, let me describe its pros and cons so you can make up your mind.

THE HIGHWAY TO WEALTH BUILDING

The average median US household income in 2018 was about $60,293.[1] The median American household currently holds about $12,330 in savings. Twenty-nine percent of households have less than $1,000 in savings, according to data collected by the Federal Reserve in October 2019.[2] Yet, millions more have little to no savings.

Outside of their home, most Americans are not investing in real estate either. Yet they should be, as it can be the highway to wealth. When you can replace your salary with passive rental income, you will enjoy the wealth that will allow you to retire comfortably. Investing in real estate is the surest and fastest way to do this. You do not need a great education or a rich father, as success in real estate depends on patience.

If you are like the average American, you most likely have little left over after paying your mortgage and living expenses. What savings you do have goes into your retirement account, or perhaps a bank account that earns you less than one percent a year.

At today's interest rate, if you began putting $100 a month into your bank, then at the end of ten years, you would have earned a measly $60.00. That is neither an incentive to save nor is it the way to become wealthy.

However, if you have good credit, you could take your small savings a long way by investing using the leverage of a mortgage loan. You could begin your career as a real estate investor with only $10,000 using an FHA mortgage, which needs just a 3.5 percent down payment. Using your $10,000 cash savings (or family loan), you could buy a $285,750 investment property.

If you continued to invest in real estate after the first investment, you would be borrowing money to grow your investments. You would also have to pay interest and principal on what you borrowed. The repayment would come out of rents from your investment property, and not out of your pocket.

As you pay your mortgage, you are decreasing the amount you owe while increasing your net worth and receiving the cash flow after your investment properties pay their expenses. Think long-term as you should with real estate investing. In thirty years, you will own a free and clear property and an appreciated asset.

BETTER RETURNS THAN THE STOCK MARKET

A tangible asset secures a real estate investment. So it is an exceptionally stable investment. Experience has proven that an investment property will hold its value and appreciate over time. If the monthly mortgage payments are paid and satisfactory insurance is placed on the property, it is unlikely that you will experience a total loss on a real estate investment. You can lose totally in the stock market.

Unlike investing in stocks, where it is risky to invest with borrowed funds, you can use significant amounts of financing when investing in real estate without adding a ton of risk.[3]

Also, with a real estate investment, your risk of loss is limited by the time you hold on to your property. As the market improves, as it always does long-term, so does the value of your real estate investment. As your value increases, so does your equity (wealth). On the other hand, stock market risk is constant because of various daily market conditions.

Stocks and bonds are subject to market risks that include events beyond an investor's control. But real estate gives you tighter control of your investment in several ways. You can leverage your property's value to take advantage of its various incomes as it appreciates.

PASSIVE INCOME SOURCE

The big advantage of real estate investing is its capacity to produce cash flow. It is the number-one reason to invest in real estate—to create a passive income to enjoy more of the life you want. The first subject you need to know about investing in real estate is cash flow. *Cash flow* is the rent that tenants are paying after you have paid all expenses and the mortgage. Cash flow is what remains for you. What is so great about cash flow is that if you bought a property properly (see Chapter 5), you would be making anywhere from 10 to 20 percent on your return. If you bought smart, you might even receive a higher yield than 20 percent just on your cash flow.

Cash flow is a considered way of receiving passive income every month. *Passive income* is defined as a stream of income earned without effort. It can be further defined as progressive passive income when there is little effort needed to grow the stream of income. Often, cash flow only strengthens as you pay down your mortgage—and build up your equity. According to Forbes, in 2020, apartments rents will continue to rise, even if home prices do not.[4]

REAL ESTATE VALUE INCREASES OVER TIME

If you take the time to check the record, you will find that history has shown the longer you keep an investment property, the more money you will make. Yes, during real estate market cycles, values can swing as they did during the 2007 housing downturn. But those that held onto their property were not affected, as the values returned and increased over what they were before 2007. The entire country is seeing a significant appreciation of real estate values.

REAL ESTATE HAS A HIGH ASSET VALUE

Look at traditional investments such as stocks and bonds. There is nothing to stop their values from dropping to zero—making them worthless certificates. However, real estate values are not affected so radically. The land will always have a value, as will your investment property. Which means there is less risk to value when you own property. It also means there is a more significant benefit to putting your money into an investment consisting of a tangible asset. Unlike with stock, you can hedge your risks by buying property insurance.

APPRECIATION OF ASSET VALUE

When you buy a property, there are two events at play. You have inflation, which means if it is higher than the interest rate you are receiving at your bank, the cash you have on deposit in the bank is losing value every day. On the other hand, you have property appreciation, which means your property is increasing in value every day. Combining the two means that when you buy a property, its worth is growing daily. The rate of real estate inflation and the general rate of inflation is almost identical.[6] That often ranges from 3 to 5 percent, which is where the real estate growth average is. Some years, it may be even more. That is on top of the return you receive from cash flow.

PRINCIPAL PAYDOWN

We mentioned taking off your mortgage from your rental income as an expense to decide cash flow. But a portion of that mortgage is paying down the principal part of your loan of what you owe on the property. In this way, paying that portion of the mortgage is like putting aside that money into a savings account. Every month the amount you owe on the property is becoming less and less. This is another automatic way that you are getting a return on your investment.

TAX SHELTERING THROUGH DEPRECIATION

Depreciation is defined as a decrease in the value of an asset over time because of wear and tear. Depreciation is a wonderful way to mitigate your overall tax load, so you will want to know exactly how it works.

You have bought a great investment property; maybe you have renovated it. The IRS schedule states that in 27 ½ years, the property will be worth zero because of age. In reality, of course, this does not happen. In time, your property should appreciate. Every year for 27 ½ years, you get to claim on your taxes an expense called depreciation, equal to 1/27 ½ of the value you paid for your rental property, plus any capital improvements.

As an example, say the value of your investment property (less land value) is $150,000. Then you would divide that value by 27 ½. That would give you a result of $5,455. This is the amount that you would get to take off on your taxes every year for the next 27 ½ years.

As an example, if your net operating income (rent minus expenses) were $5,500 for the year, you would only pay taxes on $45 ($5,500 − $5,455 = $45). This is a great way to reduce your overall tax burden and another way that real estate investments help you grow your wealth.

One caution is that you cannot depreciate the value of the land, only the value of what is built on it. So, the number you must use in the depreciation deduction is the total *improvement* value.

That is why rental income property is a better cash flow producing alternative than investing in and leasing out raw land for mobile homes. You cannot depreciate raw land; thus, you would miss the depreciation that helps you shelter your income from taxes. Raw land can be a great investment strategy, but not as good as owning rental real estate. You cannot depreciate it as, in the eyes of the IRS, land does not lose its value.

Learn about *cost segregation*.[7] This method is a sophisticated tax planning tool that allows you to hasten depreciation to improve cash flow by deferring federal and state income taxes. However, the IRS only allows a licensed accountant to perform this method. It a method you cannot do yourself.

On average, 20 to 40 percent of building structure components fall into tax categories that can be written off much quicker than the 27 ½ years allotted for the building structure. A licensed accountant does a cost segregation study, which separates costs of a property that would otherwise be depreciated over 27 ½ years for residential properties or 39 years for commercial properties. The goal of the cost segregation study is to identify all property-related costs that can be depreciated over 5, 7, and 15 years. For example, certain electrical outlets that are dedicated to equipment such as appliances or computers could be depreciated over five years.

If you have several investment properties, the cost for the study should be more than offset by the added depreciation that has been calculated. However, it may not be cost-effective for just one property.

Depreciation is significant because it helps you keep more money in your pocket instead of sending it to the federal government at tax time.

ADDED TAX BENEFITS FOR RENTAL PROPERTY OWNERSHIP

Also, the 2017 Tax Cuts and Jobs Act, which went into effect on January 1, 2018, aids landlords by providing new tax benefits. If you own a flow-through entity (also known as a pass-through business) and manage it as a sole proprietorship, limited liability company, partnership, or S corporation, you now may deduct an amount equal to twenty percent of your net rental income—as long as your total taxable annual income from all sources after deductions is less than $157,500 for singles or $315,000 for married couples who file jointly.[8]

THE RENEWABLE SOURCE OF CAPITAL

Refinancing your real estate property as it gains value provides you with a unique opportunity to gain a renewable source of capital. As your income pays the monthly mortgage payments, your loan amount is lessened, and the equity in your property increases further.

THERE IS A LOW BARRIER TO ENTRY

Deciding to invest in real estate is not as difficult as you might think. You do not need a bank full of money or, for that matter, a rich uncle, to make your first investment. That is because unlike stocks and bonds, there are many financing alternatives available. The typical way to start is with a twenty percent down payment. But there are other government programs where you can start with only 3 ½ percent of your own money. There are other choices if you cannot qualify for a traditional loan, such as non-recourse loans, hard money, or even personal loans.

CAPITAL LEVERAGING

Real estate is one of the few assets where using the bank's money could not be easier. Real estate property allows you to use borrowed money (your mortgage) to build your investment's earning potential. That feature is known as *leverage*.[9] When you use leverage, you are using borrowed capital. Since real property is a tangible asset, financing is readily available. Most banks lend money backed by real estate in the form of mortgages. The return on an investment using borrowed funds is far higher than the same investment bought for all cash.

You are further benefiting from leverage when the rental income produced by your investment property is used to pay down your mortgage. If you analyze your numbers correctly, the income you receive from your property investment should be enough. It should be enough to cover your mortgage payments and all property expenses for each rental unit.

INCREASING EQUITY BY PROPERTY IMPROVEMENTS

In its 2017 fourth-quarter report, the Federal Reserve Bank of St. Louis showed the average home equity surpassed its prerecession peak of $13,431.94, reaching a new high of $14,416.75.[10] As you pay down your mortgage, you are increasing the equity in your property. However, making property improvements can also increase the value of your property. Alterations, such as painting or changing light fixtures, do not have to be expensive.

If you are planning on improving to increase property values, you should do so, as they pay off. The only caution you will want to take is not to over-improve. Here are some typical improvements that will provide you with a high return:

> **Small updates.** This update provides the highest return on investment for a rehabilitation project. Fresh paint will renew any room and make it sparkle. Think about painting the ceiling as well. Pay attention to the trim and baseboard as these show their age sooner than most areas of a room.

> **Colors set the mood**. Use a classic pallet such as white or off-white. Stay away from yellows, which make the walls look dingy. If you stay with one color, it will make future touch-ups simpler.

> **Boost curb appeal.** Renters are different from homebuyers in several ways, but one way in which they are the same is both want an attractive place to live. Great curb appeal makes a difference; everyone—renters and potential homebuyers—will want to see what is inside. Redo house numbers, change the entry door lockset,

and add a wall-mounted mailbox and an overhead light fixture. All these will add style and curb appeal.

Update flooring. Carpeting is not a good idea in rental properties. It is incredibly high maintenance, readily shows wear, and often needs to be replaced with each new tenant. If you can, install hardwood floors. They are not as expensive as you may think. You will gain several advantages. They will make the property appear high-end and, more importantly, need little maintenance and will last twenty years. If expensive hardwood busts the budget, consider simulated hardwood in vinyl as an alternative.

Add a kitchen backsplash. Adding a backsplash in the kitchen is inexpensive and easy. It will make the property appear upscale and will keep it cleaner and more sanitary. A tile backsplash needs just a wipe to keep it clean and neat. Use a subway tile for a classic look that never gets old and use a gray grout for added contrast. Subway tile is inexpensive, too.

Replace switches, receptacles, and plates. Replace old-fashioned toggle switches with the more modern rocker switches. It is an inexpensive way to modernize a kitchen or any room for that matter—change receptacles and all switches and receptacle plates to bring the property up to the twenty-first-century look. Add the proper USB receptacle in the kitchen. Spend an afternoon and a few hundred dollars on this upgrade as it will make a visual difference.

Add new window coverings. Change out those old-fashioned one-inch blinds. For a bit more, you can add simulated wood two-inch blinds. It makes a big difference and adds an upgraded look to any room.

HEDGE AGAINST INFLATION

History has proven the value of real estate has increased at a similar rate to inflation. That is because of the positive relationship between GDP growth and the demand for real estate. As the economy expands, the need for real estate drives rents higher. Thus, a long-term real estate investing plan provides an excellent hedge against inflation. This asset will keep your standard of living and increase your wealth.

YOU CAN USE YOUR TAX-DEFERRED RETIREMENT ACCOUNT

Did you know that your Individual Retirement Account (IRA) or 401(k) can be used to invest in real estate? The IRS allows individuals to add retirement funds in real estate. It is an excellent tax savings because buying your investment property through an IRA enables you to take advantage of all the tax savings these accounts offer.

You will need to consult a tax professional, though, as the language about an IRA real estate investment must be correctly titled. Some choices allow you to include using undivided interest and partnering with others. Using your retirement account, the profits you earn on your real estate investments can be largely shielded from tax liability—just another reason to choose real estate as your preferred investment vehicle.

Caution: Though we may have given you optimism about using your IRA for real estate investment, there are a few caveats to consider:

- Mortgage loans must be non-recourse.
- Your IRA may be subject to an unrelated business income tax (UBIT), according to Section 511 of the Internal Revenue Code.
- All expenses related to property owned by your self-directed IRA (maintenance, improvements, property taxes, condo association fees, general bills, and the like, must be paid from your IRA.
- All income produced by property owned by your self-directed IRA must be paid into your IRA.
- You and your IRA are two separate entities, the investment needs to be titled in the name of your IRA—not to you personally.

YOUR INVESTMENT IS A FORCED RETIREMENT PLAN

Americans are saving less than ever because of rising costs and stagnant salaries. Though the 2008 economic crisis is blamed, data shows that Americans have been saving less for some time now.

Many people lack the self-discipline to add to an IRA or 401(k). But with the purchase of a rental property, the saving is forced as equality builds, and the mortgage is reduced month after month. If you bought one rental property a year, you would not get rich overnight. By taking the time to build a diverse portfolio, you would be steadily increasing your wealth.

DIVERSIFYING

If you are a stock investor, adding investment real estate to your portfolio helps offset the market volatility of other high-risk assets. It lessens the risk of your family portfolio and provides you with more reliable returns.

WEALTH CREATION

In time, carefully chosen real estate properties will be a powerful asset that will build your wealth. Your mortgage loans will continue to decrease as you make monthly payments, while the real estate property appreciates because of inflation. The formula produces increased equity and personal wealth.

This simple wealth-building equation works like this:

Investment Value Appreciation
+ Mortgage Loan Reduction
= Wealth Creation

CONSIDER THE DRAWBACKS OF OWNING RENTAL PROPERTIES

The thought of investing in a single-family home or duplex to have rent-paying tenants may sound attractive. For many investors, it is. But investing in real estate for cash flow and long-term capital appreciation does come with risk. For example, the housing market does rise and fall depending on location, supply and demand, and the economy. Not everyone can manage property and tenants, either.

Time-consuming. A significant risk that many people miss is that real estate needs much time to conduct research. It is not something you can go into casually and expect immediate results and returns. As you will see in the book, it takes work to research the market and properties. Once you buy a property, if you do not use a property management firm, you must be involved with tenant administration, marketing, and maintenance issues.

Lack of liquidity. Real estate is an illiquid asset. Even in the most active seller's market, it can take several months to complete a sale. If you need to sell fast, chances are you will not sell at the best price.

Rising taxes and insurance premiums. Though your mortgage interest and principal may be fixed, consider that taxes could grow faster than you can increase rents. Insurance premiums may also increase more rapidly than expected because of a natural disaster.

Difficult tenants. Despite your best efforts in screening tenants, you could wind up with a difficult one. For example, they could be demanding or late payers, forget to turn off the water, and so on. Or they could cause property damage. That is what security deposits are for.

Neighborhood decline. Your property should thrive among other well-maintained homes as local amenities improve. The result will lead to significant cash flow with stable costs. However, neighborhoods in decline can reverse your fortunes. Stay aware of the local politics where you invest. With a watchful eye, you can lessen this issue.

Changes to tax code. The tax code continues to change. Pay attention to whether it changes in ways that would either reduce or remove some or all the tax benefits for homeownership and flow-through businesses.

Landlord role. Not everyone is cut out to be a landlord. You may not feel comfortable about rent increases or you may not be protective of the way others treat your property, which can lead to conflicts. In the end, you must be firm about rent increases and property care. If not, you could wind up collecting rent that is well below market price or leaves the property undervalued.

Property Maintenance. Keeping current with repairs is the key to management. You might be able to do some work yourself. However, most owners lack the time, tools, or skills for home repair. Expect to incur costs for hiring plumbers, electricians, and other contractors.

ADDITIONAL FACTORS TO CONSIDER

When it comes to stocks versus investment properties, purchasing property often needs more capital. The advantage of property assets buying is the buyer has high leverage. Meaning the buyer can borrow much of the purchase price and only use a small amount of his capital.

For example, investing $20,000 into stocks buys $20,000 worth. However, the same investment using an 80 percent mortgage in real estate could buy $100,000 in property with a loan providing tax-deductible interest.

The rent produced from the investment should pay the mortgage and other expenses. Also, if effectively managed, the property should throw off cash flow above its costs. Besides the cash flow, the property provides the investor with depreciation benefits that shelter income and other tax write-offs.

Another advantage of a real estate investment over securities is that in a sale, capital gains taxes can be deferred in something called a 1031 exchange in the IRS tax code.

IT IS A BUYER'S MARKET

We can thank the recession that caused the real estate bubble to burst. It has provided an excellent opportunity to invest in rental real estate. There are even real estate opportunities created by turnkey operators that have taken all the work out, offering investment possibilities around the country. Here is why we believe it is a buyer's market in 2020.

> **Low mortgage rates are back.** Not long ago, mortgages rates hit an all-time low. When they did, the market exploded with home buyers and real estate investors. Unfortunately, that led to many people over-leveraging, which in turn resulted in the market's collapse. As an investor, you should learn from this lesson and not overborrow because you do not want to wind up in a similar predicament.
>
> **Anticipated foreclosures.** RealtyTrac® reports that as of March 2020, 335,309 properties in the US are in some stage of foreclosure (default, auction, or bank-owned). The total quantity of homes listed for sale on RealtyTrac total 764,312.[11] According to data supplied by CoreLogic, nearly 1 in every 25 Americans was behind on their mortgage in May 2019. Due to the job losses resulting from the coronavirus, it is anticipated that there will be many more foreclosures during 2021. And more will fall behind at some point in their homeownership. RealtyTrac lists the top five states for foreclosures by the fraction of properties for sale that are in some stage of foreclosure:
>
> | | |
> |---|---|
> | Delaware – | 1 in every 2715 |
> | Maryland – | 1 in every 3792 |
> | Illinois – | 1 in every 5340 |
> | Connecticut – | 1 in every 5503 |
> | Florida – | 1 in every 6112 [5] |

Delaware has the nation's highest availability of foreclosed properties, with 84,442 properties valued from $100–$200,000.

Predominant preference for houses. According to the Pew Research Center, more US households are headed by renters than at any point since 1965. The desire for homeownership has decreased over time. Instead, people have turned toward renting.[13] But they are not just renting because they cannot buy. They are making this choice because it affords them better personal and financial opportunities. According to the Zillow Group Report on Consumer Housing Trends, twelve percent of repeat buyers are seriously considering renting their next home instead of buying it.[14]

Now, when it comes to the choice of a house over an apartment rental, most seekers would choose the house. This is especially true for past homeowners. These tenants will take care of your rental investment as if it were their own because they appreciate owning their own home.

Tenants prefer private over corporate landlords. There is something to say for private landlords over property management companies. They care more about their property and provide more personal service. They provide a more secure feeling in that it is only they who have a key to the home. Tenants renting from a private landlord will have had direct contact with the landlord. As a result, most renters prefer them.

Real estate prices are low. Not every market is inexpensive, especially those found on both coasts. However, in the Midwest and South, prices are low. That is especially so in states such as Florida, Michigan, Ohio, Indiana, Texas, Indiana, and Nevada. If you are not located in one of these states, you might want to consider the many turnkey rental investment companies that would be happy to explore an investment there.

Short sales opportunities. A short sale sells for less than is owed on the mortgage but needs approval from the seller's mortgage lender. Gaining support often takes several months. A short sale is a much better choice than buying at a foreclosure sale. With a foreclosure, you never know the condition of the property until you buy it, whereas a short sale buy allows you to conduct the traditional inspections that you would under a normal for-sale listing. A short sale will enable you to purchase at an excellent price.

Great long-term investment. Real estate is the best long-term investment for most people. If you look back over a thirty-year history, you will prove to you that today's property values are far greater than they were. Add to that higher value that your tenants are paying all your expenses, and the deal gets even sweeter.

SUMMARY

Yes, this book is about the benefits of real estate investing. There are drawbacks, as nothing is perfect. The major one is real estate's lack of liquidity. Unlike stocks and bonds, it is rather challenging to convert a real estate asset into cash and cash into an asset. A real estate transaction can take months to close.

But after reviewing the risks of real estate investment, we see that its benefits far outweigh the risks of ownership. We have shown you the many reasons you should invest in real estate: passive income, appreciation, hedge against inflation, tax benefits, and its capacity to make you wealthy over time. There is great evidence that a well-structured real estate investment can be one of the best choices for your money. If you are convinced of the benefits to you and your family and want to invest in real estate, but you don't know where to start, this book can make you an investor in as little as ninety days.

Many before you have built their multimillion-dollar real estate empires by investing in rental real estate just like you can. So, you can rest assured that this book will help you get the ball rolling on your way to your real estate successes!

KEY TAKEAWAYS

- Most real estate investors make money through rental income, appreciation, and profits produced by activities related to income-producing property.
- There are many benefits to investing in real estate, including passive income, stable cash flow, tax advantages, diversification, and leverage.
- Real estate is not a liquid asset, and therefore, needs research, money, and time. But it provides a passive income and the potential for large appreciation.
- Comparing the returns of real estate and the stock market is an apples-to-oranges comparison—the causes that affect prices, values, and profits are distinct.

NEXT STEPS

In the next chapter, you will learn how to select the best type of real estate that makes sense for a beginner. You will see how the best investment type also depends on you, your ambitions, and what you are attracted to. We will explore the many types of investment available to you. By the end of the chapter, you should have discovered the perfect investment that makes you excited and ready to learn how to buy it in the following sections.

CHAPTER THREE

SELECTING YOUR BEST INVESTMENT TYPE

Now, one thing I tell everyone is learn about real estate. Repeat after me: real estate provides the highest returns, the greatest values and the least risk.

—Armstrong Williams

John Jacob Astor, one of history's famous financiers, was reputed to be the richest man in the country during his day. It was reported that once Astor sold a lot near Wall Street for $8,000. The buyer, confident that he had outsmarted Astor, could not resist a little self-congratulation after signing the papers. "Why in a few years this lot will be worth twelve thousand dollars," he gloated. "True," said Astor, "But with your eight thousand, I will buy eighty lots above Canal Street, and by the time your lot is worth twelve thousand dollars, my eighty lots will be worth eighty thousand dollars."[1]

Astor's investment choice was raw land around New York City. He would pick up vacant plots of land from the city and leave them undeveloped or unmaintained. Astor's appetite for New York real estate appears to have had no limits. On his deathbed in 1848, he said, "Could I begin life again, knowing what I now know, and had money to invest; I would buy every foot of land on the island of Manhattan."[2]

Astor's approach to investing was the opposite of complexity. He would simply buy or, at times, lease land. In turn, he would then rent it to developers whose projects he sometimes financed. Much of his fortune came from buying vast tracts of land, which he subdivided into smaller lots. He would then lease out the lots for short periods.

Real estate can be considered the oldest asset class. This fact is a given to most beginning investors. What they do not realize is just how many asset subclasses make up real estate. In Astor's case, he favored the simplest of all forms of real estate—raw land.

THE BEST REAL ESTATE FOR YOU

But as you explore the variety of asset types and understand more about them, you will be surprised to find investors who earned their wealth specializing in many other niches. This chapter should answer your question—What is the best real estate investment for you?

As with Astor, buying properties and expecting prices to climb has only one exit strategy: sell later. Unfortunately, there is only one way to be successful with this asset group: hope the property continues to appreciate. Any other results other than appreciating and selling are guaranteed to lose money. When the market dived into the last real estate crisis, these land investors lost their shirts. All real estate assets dropped in value, then, but was it the fault of real estate?

Experienced investors do not rely on the hope of appreciation. They purchase properties that produce cash flow, property that will produce more income than it costs to own. These folks who can show positive "cash flow" do not care what the market does. If prices drop, they are safe. If prices rise, they have more options.[3]

SELECTING THE BEST REAL ESTATE INVESTMENT

Even with that in mind, there is no best type. Instead, there is the type that best fits your circumstances and what you wish to achieve. However, since we are focusing on getting started within the first ninety days, we will concentrate on a single-family or duplex rental property. It will best answer your ninety-day investment challenge as there are millions of them, making them easier for you to find and buy.

However, you should understand all your choices as an investor. That is why we will go over them. No matter which investment type you eventually select, the importance of location cannot be overemphasized. Location is so important that we have devoted an entire chapter to cover the subject.

The investment type also depends on you, your ambitions, and what you are attracted to. If you are strongly attracted to vacant land, you will be more motivated to study it. With your new knowledge, you can be more successful in that type of investment. If your preference is to be more actively involved with your real estate investment, you might be more attracted to land development or property rehabbing. On the other hand, if you wish for a more passive role, then rental properties should be your top choice.

You do not have to invest in just one property class, either. Investment diversity is a great way to mitigate risk. You can be successful in various real estate property types. You can start with residential rentals, and then as you gain experience, it will be natural for you to move on to commercial properties.

No matter which real estate investment you choose, there are four ways you can make money with it.

Real estate appreciation. Appreciation, or increase in value, occurs when a property's asset value grows because of growth in the real estate market and inflation. For example, as property rents increase, so does the value of the property. If there are significant developments nearby, it also may increase property values. If you add amenities to the property, this may cause its value to increase. That is what appreciation is. But appreciation is not a predictable commodity and cannot be relied on as well as cash flow, making it the riskier reason for investment.

Cash flow income. Cash flow is the measure of cash income produced by an investment property. It is the result of the rental earnings from tenants of an income property investment less its expenses. Other types of investments, such as storage units, office buildings, retail establishments, and Airbnb rentals, can produce cash flow.

Ancillary real estate investment income. Ancillary real estate investment income is income generated within an income property. It might include coin-operated laundry machines or vending machines—all captive money-making centers for owners.

Depreciation. Depreciation is a phantom expense that can be used as a deduction on your taxes. Thus, it leaves you more income, which you can reinvest to produce even more income.

TYPES OF REAL ESTATE INVESTMENT PROPERTIES TO CONSIDER

For real estate investing for beginners, choosing the investment to start with is especially important but is often confusing. Choosing the wrong kinds of investment may prove difficult to manage or, worse, an investment that winds up losing money. You can avoid these mistakes by understanding the pros and cons of the various investment types.

- Single-family – owner-occupied
- Single-family – rentals
- Multiple-family home
- Vacant land

SINGLE-FAMILY HOMES

Real estate investors have been arguing for years about what is the best rental property. While there are several alternatives, each having its drawbacks, a beginning investor will find the most benefits with single-family homes. And if you are starting with little money, single-family homes should be your first choice. That is because there are many government-backed and traditional mortgages available with low-down payments. But these mortgages are offered only on owner-occupied properties.

Also, single-family homes are more affordable than other types of investment properties, hands down. Just look at the listing prices for single-family homes compared to multi-family houses. You will see the difference.

A single-family house's purchase price is usually lower, and the expense of a single-family rental is smaller. A smaller property often equates to lower costs for maintenance and repairs. There is no common area as there would be with a duplex or triplex, which means that expense is eliminated. With a single-family home, tenants take better care of the property. That just might be psychological as a single-family house tenant may feel that it is more like home than they would in a small apartment. In a single-unit rental, even property management is less expensive.

There are other benefits to a single-family investment as well. For example, tax deductions are more substantial, and the depreciation period is longer. You can take depreciation for 27½ years compared to 39 years for commercial properties (like multi-family homes with more than four housing units). This means that you will be receiving higher cash flow from a single-family investment per square foot.

A smaller single renter's investment property will have lower property taxes and insurance costs, as well as a lesser mortgage loan with lower interest.

Because of these benefits, a single-family home is the best choice for investors with limited funds. Thus, it is the best choice for the first investment purchase. It is affordable, and the more inexpensive the investment property, the more properties can be purchased by an investor to expand their investment portfolio and increase overall rental income and return on investment.

LENDERS FAVOR SINGLE FAMILY HOMES

Another reason for choosing single-family investments is that first-time investors can often find it difficult to receive financing on non-owner-occupied properties. It is far easier to get the funding on a single-family home with little cash down through a choice of government-backed lending programs.

Banks and credit unions are in business to make loans on single-family homes. They view them as a low-risk investment. Traditionally, a single-family home has remained a stable investment in most markets throughout the country. They consistently hold property value over the long-term.

Though they may decline in value during a recession, they almost always bounce back when the recession ends. Since mortgage lenders are in the business to lend on single-family homes, they offer their lowest interest rates. That translates to more income for the investor.

What is the best single-family home investment? As you will learn in the chapter on financial analysis, it is the property with the best numbers. It will show excellent cash-on-cash return on an outstanding potential rent. It will have a reasonable cap rate (more about this later) and a good return on investment.

Where does a new real estate investor look for low-risk single-family homes which will attract mortgage lenders? Chapter Four, *How to Find Deals*, will show you.

MULTI-FAMILY HOMES

A duplex home is also a great way to start as a beginner. Because most lenders want owner-occupied homes to qualify for a mortgage, a duplex property provides both worlds. While you live on one side of the house, your tenant will help pay your mortgage and expenses with his rent. Now I know we just finished recommending a single-family home as an investment. But a duplex house, though a two-unit home, is still considered a residential home by many lenders. Investing in one can put you well on your way toward commercial real estate investing.

VACANT LAND

Many investors neglect to consider vacant land, but it can be an excellent investment following Mr. Astor's model. Vacant land is inexpensive, and except for taxes, it has low to no operating costs. Property taxes assessed to vacant land are also the lowest of any real estate investment. Even though taxes may add up over time, they should only be thousands of dollars. It is easily recouped on the sale of the land. As an investment property, if bought in the right location, the property can be leased to farming enterprises, hunters, or loggers.

If there is any real risk to land buying, it is finding lenders willing to lend on raw land. It often means that land is a cash purchase requiring that a buyer has large amounts of cash for raw land transactions.

As was discussed earlier, real estate demands good local knowledge. It is especially important when considering a land purchase as you will need to know about the regional market economics and development if you wish to make a future profit. If the area has a possibility for future growth, then the land that is being considered might be a very profitable investment where large gains could be realized sometime in the future.

To own the right piece of land bought at the right price provides extraordinary stability and peace of mind. You cannot afford to overlook raw land in your search for the correct real estate investment.

Real estate investing experts say that land is a unique asset class that needs careful investigation and due diligence. Though there may be advantages, market trends are unpredictable, and there are few opportunities to earn income from vacant land. So, it can be a risky investment.

If you buy the property to develop it, then look for ways to earn money from it. For example, you could lease it for agriculture, self-storage, parking, billboards, or a communications tower.

Know that land purchase needs careful consideration and planning.

- You do not need to "do" anything to vacant land
- Land is a "hands-off" investment
- Owners of vacant land are often motivated to sell
- Land investors have few competitors
- After learning how to research, you can often buy vacant land without seeing it

There are many strategies used to invest in land. But the top three are used most often.

Buy and hold. This is often the slowest way to profit. It is buying and then waiting until the market grows more robust so you can sell for more than you paid for it.

Transitional buying. This is buying the land to transition it to its highest and best use. It is a big market. The property will usually cost more, but if it pays off, you can profit greatly.

Purchase to lease. Leasing the land you buy will provide steady cash flow. Leasing your property to users such as hunters and farmers needs more marketing work. But it can pay off.

Drawbacks of Land Investment

Although there are benefits to raw land investing, there are also large risks.

Taxes can be an issue. There are different taxes in counties and areas to contend with.

Previous land uses. Past uses will affect the land's value and how it can be used in the future. Environmental hazards could destroy the land's value. But it is often challenging to conduct a historical records search.

Lack of patience. Returns on investment often take years, needing patience by the land investor. The rule is that you should only invest money into land that you will not need for a while. *Good things come in time* is the credo of land investors.

Turnkey Rental Properties

Due to the growing interest in real estate investment, many beginning investors are finding that they are being priced out of the investment market. The development of turnkey rental investments offer could the answer for some. It is an alternative to the traditional direct ownership rental model and can produce a cash flow.

Across the country, third-party turnkey providers have been proving themselves to meet the unanswered demand. Is this a good idea or just a marketing gimmick to wrestle away new investors' hard-earned money? Let us examine this niche market.

First, we should more fully understand the term "turnkey rental properties." It can be defined as a newer investment idea where one party buys and rehabilitates the property, then uses a third-party management company to rent it and tend to its future operations. Once the property is up and running, it is sold to a new investor, or rented with little need for hands-on management. As a new investor, this is how you might work with these types of companies:

Locating a property. After contacting a turnkey company, you would discuss property types, locations, and investment goals. Larger turnkey operations have listings of established turnkey investments for you to evaluate.

Financing considerations. The turnkey company is usually prepared to offer the new investor several investment alternatives that a new investor may not be familiar with. New investors may not know about loan types such as FHA, VA, or conventional low-down loans. They also may not know about funding using their 401(k) or property exchanges. Financing methods is one of the advantages that this organization can offer.

Purchasing the property. Turnkey providers are end-to-end service providers that specialize in working with long-distance sellers. After you have made your property selection, they will arrange to help you complete all the documents of that state as well as all inspections, appraisals, lender documents, and anything else needed to close on the property.

Rehabbing the property. As turnkey might suggest, all properties have been brought up to code and put into a condition whereby they can place a renter. This means that some properties need major rehabilitation while others not so much. The result is the new investors have nothing to do, as the turnkey provider does all the work.

Property management. The benefit of turnkey investing is that you have a company that promises to do all the management for you. The company does the tenant management, from screening to rent collections. They take care of the maintenance issues, so an investor will not get a weekend call. They provide monthly rent with the rent checks for the investor to deposit.

Fees and charges. Of course, they are charges for these services. Typically, they average about 3 percent for the property buy. Think of it as a real estate agent's fee. There is a monthly charge between 7 and 10 percent for property management.

There are many hundreds of turnkey firms scattered throughout the country. None of them work the same. So, our descriptions are general. While some companies provide the entire process including acquisition, rehabilitation, management, and sale to the investors, others are set up to help the investors locate inexpensive properties that need rehabbing, which the company will finish for the investor. Since the range of services can vary so much, it is best to research each company you are interested in. We have provided a list of some of the top turnkey companies in Table 1.

TOP TURNKEY COMPANIES IN 2020

Turnkey Real Estate Companies	Markets They Serve
Bric Group	FL, TX
Home Union	AL, CA, FL, GA, IN, IL, NC, NV, OH, MO, TX
Howard Hanna	MD, MI, NC, NY, OH, PA, VA, WV
JWB Real Estate Capital	FL
Maverick Investor Group	IN, IL, MO, OH
Memphis Invest	AR, MO, OK, TN, TX
Meridian Pacific Properties	MS, TN
NextGen Invest	OH
Norada Real Estate Investments	AL, AR, FL, GA, ID, IL, IN, MO, MS, OH, OK, TN, TX, UT, WI
Prime Properties	TX
Roofstock	AL, AR, AZ, CA, DE, FL, GA, IL, IN, MI, MN, MO, MS, NC, NJ, NV, OH, OK, PA, SC, TN, TX, WI
Spartan Invest	AL
Turnkey Properties	AR, TN

Table 1. Listing of the top turnkey real estate companies as of 2020

BENEFITS OF
TURNKEY RENTAL
INVESTMENTS

1 LOW PURCHASE PRICES

Turnkey companies offer affordable investments averaging from $50,000 to $150,000

2 FINANCING EXPERTISE

Turnkey companies advise on optimum financing alternatives to provide investor with the best financing for the purchase

3 LOCATION FINDER

Turnkey company has identified **appropriate locations** to provide investor with good cash on cash returns and monthly cash flows saving investor time

4 CURATED INVESTMENTS

Chose from listings of rehabbed and tenanted investment rental properties – that already cash flow

5 PURCHASING ADVISORY

Turnkey companies arrange inspections, appraisals, contracts and similar for a smooth investor purchasing experience

6 WORRY FREE MANAGEMENT

Your investment will be managed by a third-party management company that rents, repairs and keeps tenants happy

Figure 3. Benefits of Turnkey Rental Investments

POPULARITY OF TURNKEY RENTAL PROPERTIES

The attraction to turnkey rentals, especially among new investors, is because of their lower cost and ease of ownership because of the elimination of management. Turnkey properties range in price from $50,000 to $150,000. They are usually located in those markets hit hardest by the 2017 real estate bubble, such as the Carolinas, Tennessee, Florida, Georgia, and Ohio.[4]

According to RealtyTrac.com, the average landlord of a single-family home in suburban Atlanta sees a 25.8 percent gross annual yield, a measure of yearly rent divided by median sales price. It does not include other potential costs. This is compared to a 3.4 percent yield in the San Francisco Bay Area, where the median home price was $675,000, as reported by data provider CoreLogic.[5]

Turnkey opportunities sound too good to be valid for a new investor. You plop your money down and wham, you are in the investing business with a tenant you never met and expect to never hear from again. However, long-distance investing has a downside. If you are unfamiliar with an area, you will not know about vacancy rates or whether you need special insurance for tornadoes or hurricanes. You will not see until it is too late if the local government is discussing elevating properties in the area due to past flooding and similar costly issues.

TURNKEY INVESTMENT DANGERS

Turnkey investments are typically marketed to uninformed investors. They sell the proposition of worry-free investing with a nice monthly payout. Because of this and the fact that most of these buyers are from out of the area, they often fail to do the proper due diligence or any background research at all. They are drawn in by the well-crafted marketing materials, only to feel buyer's remorse soon after the closing is over.

Uneducated buyers assume turnkey means that you do not have to do a thing. This mistaken belief touted in the marketing literature promises that someone else does the buying, renovating, leasing, and management. You are lulled in believing that all you must do is deposit rent checks. Now, that can be true with some of the more established companies. But many turnkey investment providers sell people on the fact that the homes have already been renovated when that is not the case. Be careful. Due to the proliferation of turnkey organizations, many of them are more Internet marketing companies as opposed to real estate companies. So, buyer beware and do your due diligence.[6]

SHOULD YOU INVEST IN A TURNKEY RENTAL INVESTMENT?

As you have read so far, there are many real estate investment choices. In the end, of course, it is your decision. But we advise you to base your investment decision on what you learn from studying local markets and the objectives of your investment strategy. As for turnkey rental investment, it just may be the right choice for you if you have found that your market prices prevent adequate NOI and cash flow.

That means that you must be cautious about where and with whom you invest your money. If you are going to make a turnkey investment, make sure you visit the property, give it your inspection, and meet the turnkey company personnel before you buy.

Turnkey properties are straightforward to buy. But, as with all real estate properties, they are more complicated to sell. Make sure you negotiate an escape plan with your turnkey company in case things do not work out.

ADVANTAGES OF DUPLEX INVESTING

If you are considering a duplex investment, then the easiest way to finance it is with a federally backed FHA mortgage. It needs a lower minimum down payment (3½ percent) and allows for credit scores lower than many conventional loans. Most real estate investment properties would not qualify for this desirable financing. For example, a multi-family home with four or more units is not eligible, even if it is owner-occupied. However, a duplex property does if one unit is owner-occupied. By using an FHA loan for a single-family home, you would lose a year's worth of rental income before legally being able to vacate the property and find tenants. The good news is the investor needs only to occupy the property for twelve months. After that time, with a duplex, the unit can be rented out so the property has two rent-paying tenants. By beginning with a duplex as your first investment, you will also have hands-on experience of dealing with a tenant. This experience will be helpful as you invest in more properties. Creative investing begins with a multi-family purchase. That is because using the FHA loan, you are investing with almost no money down. Then you are receiving income while living rent-free (or almost rent-free) in one of the units as the other tenant is helping to pay your mortgage.

DOUBLE YOUR RENTAL INCOME AFTER ONE YEAR

There is no other real estate investment that can so easily double your income in one year. Since the FHA loan only needs that you live in the property for a year, you can begin to look for your next investment meanwhile. When you move out, you will rent the vacant unit and receive an income from both apartments. It increases your income and allows you to qualify for another investment property financing loan after another year.

THE OWNER-OCCUPIED DUPLEX INVESTMENT STRATEGY

Compared to a single-family investment, a two-family property might be the most worthwhile for you. If your first investment uses a conventional mortgage, you would need to put down at least 15 to 20 percent depending on the lender and your credit score. It would most likely limit the cash that you might use for a second investment.

The better alternative would be the FHA loan with only a 3½ percent down payment. This mortgage means that you must live in the house for at least twelve months. But lenders want to see at least two years of rental history, plus management experience, before approving you for a second loan to buy another property. Because of this two-year wait, your investing progress will be substantially slowed. Living in the single-family house for a year means that you miss a year's worth of rent. To frustrate your plans, you must wait another two years to build a rental history before you can apply for another loan for the next investment. It is one of the most common mistakes made by novice real estate investors.

The correct method for the best investment strategy is to buy a two-family house using the low-down-payment FHA mortgage. You must live in one unit as you would a single-family home, but with this alternative, you have a tenant to help pay the expenses. Then once the year is up, you double your income by renting the second unit. With this method, it will only be another year for you to qualify for the two years of rental history to secure another FHA loan.

MAKE MORE RENTAL INCOME

Duplex property with both units rented usually commands higher rents than a single-family house or an apartment building. The duplex offers a tenant a backyard, a lawn, a driveway, and the feeling of more privacy than an apartment. So, tenants are willing to pay more rent for added aesthetics. Because a duplex house usually has a backyard, a driveway, and maybe even a lawn, tenants are willing to pay more in rent.

Because an owner lives in the property, tenants are usually on their best behavior. It lessens such tenant issues as disturbances and property damage. Tenants are more often on time with their rent with the owner living just next door.

PROPERTY MANAGEMENT EXPERIENCE

A big advantage of a duplex property as your first investment is that you will learn about property management and tenant administration. It will also give you time to educate yourself on leases, rent collection, property rules, and tenant notices. This is especially essential knowledge as you begin to build your property investment portfolio. A duplex house can be an excellent real estate investment for beginners. By conducting property management yourself, you can avoid paying fees to professional property managers.

THE DISADVANTAGES OF DUPLEX INVESTING

As with any tenanted investment property, finding the right tenants is critical to a successful investment. However, there is nothing certain in life, which means that you may wind up with a bad tenant no matter how well you screen them. If you are living next to such a tenant, you must face them regularly. It is not fun living next to someone disturbing the peace or not picking up their trash. Screening for good tenants takes experience and is another subject for discussion.

Though not exactly a disadvantage of duplex ownership, it is a disadvantage to your time. That is because finding a worthwhile duplex investment takes time and patience, much more than finding a single-family house. It needs more patience on your part.

IS THE DUPLEX PROPERTY THE RIGHT INVESTMENT FOR YOU?

We have described how a multi-family might just be the right investment for you to begin with. The risk to this investment is small, and what risks there are can be avoided with proper due diligence. As with a single-family investment, a duplex property, if bought using FHA financing, can be financed with only 3½ percent down. Its income for the first year should offset the expenses, and in the second year, its revenue can double so you can begin investing in another property shortly after that. So, you see, a duplex home can be an excellent start for you to invest in.

MORE EXPENSIVE THAN SINGLE-FAMILY HOMES

When doing a side-by-side comparison of multiple-family to single-family, you will see the former investment is more expensive. The multiple family is built to house more than one family and, thus, has more square feet. However, that is not the main reason for the cost difference. Single-family and multiple family are valued altogether differently. For an investor, the multiple family's values are based on its cap rate. But for a single-family home, it is based entirely on market causes.

INCREASED MAINTENANCE COST

Single-family homes are less expensive than multi-family homes, and they are less costly to maintain, too. That is because there is only one of an item to maintain. In a two-family, you have two of everything, and the single-family has no common area, as does the duplex. It is common for the tenant of a single-family home to pay utilities, landscaping, and snow removal. They also usually take better care of the property, thus lessening maintenance costs.

GREATER TAX DEDUCTIONS

Single-family homes also carry a lower property tax and insurance rate. This translates to lower overall expenses for a single-family home compared with a duplex. There is also a shorter period of depreciation for a single-family home, 27.5 years compared with 39 years for a multi-family home of over four units, which means added cash flow.

EASIER TO FINANCE

A single-family home is easier to finance as lenders look at this property type as a lower risk. That is because it offers a more stable asset whose value remains constant or appreciates over time. It is precisely the investment that lenders are seeking. Lenders are more prone to allow lower down payments, lower interest rates, no balloon payment, and even higher loan-to-value ratios.

HIGHER PROPERTY VALUE

Unlike multi-family homes, whose value is based on the net operating income, single-family houses are not valued that way. Single-family homes are traditionally not evaluated based on cash flow. An investor would find it challenging to increase the value of a multi-family property as it means raising the rents or cutting expenses. To raise the value of a single-family home, all it might need are cosmetic repairs, as the location decides its overall value.

For a single-family investor, this means thorough research to find a lower-priced neighborhood, but one that is well located and commands higher rents. They exist. You will just have to find them. An interesting phenomenon that works in an investor's favor is that an owner-occupier will place a lower value on their property to speed a sale. That enables an investor to buy at a price below the market and resell at a profit.

Because single-family value is not based on income, it will tend to appreciate faster. That is due to supply and demand.

EASE OF MANAGEMENT

A single-family home is perhaps the easiest of all real estate investments to manage, next to vacant land. Single-family tenants move less often than multi-family tenants. They also are more prompt with rent payment and take care of the property better. There are also none of those tenant disputes that you find with apartment ownership. The low turnover equates to lower operating costs.

SELLING IS EASIER

There are more buyers for single-family properties than multi-family ones. That is because the demand for single-family homes is higher than for multi-family homes. There is also a larger buyer pool, as well as more loan types available to single-family buyers.

If you are considering single-family investments, they are a popular choice for many beginning investors. They are the most common real estate type to buy and to sell. You are making it a low-risk investment. Property management is small, and expenses are low. If you want to get going but are not confident about what your investment strategy should be, consider a single-family house.

YOUR TARGET MARKET ROI

Because of market conditions across the country, not every market will provide acceptable ROIs. An investor's target cash on cash return should range between 12 and 15 percent or more. If the performance is less than that, then you should move on to the next potential investment. There will be much more on financial analysis further on in chapter six.

As to a target ROI calculation, you must combine cash flow with projected appreciation, the yearly mortgage decrease plus appreciation. That should give you an ROI target of around 20 percent. To help in the appreciation calculation, you can use the data from the U.S. Census Bureau, which shows that since 1963, real estate has appreciated, on average, 5.4 percent year after year.[7]

As an example, suppose you bought an investment property using a 20 percent down payment of $25,000 in cash. Your minimum cash on cash return target range should be $3,000 to $3,750. Then with 20 percent down, your ROI cash target should be $5,000 (25,000 x 20% = $5,000).

Keeping within these limits will assure you investment winners. But not all markets produce such results. You must be patient and thorough in your search if you want to succeed.

THE BEST MARKETS FOR RENTAL INVESTMENT PROPERTIES

No investment property is a slam dunk. That includes rentals. You could find yourself in a situation where the need for rentals is low and will stay low. You could find there are not enough tenants seeking apartment renters at the rents you need. Worse, you could overpay for your property because of a market boom.

Currently, markets such as San Francisco, Seattle, Denver, and Miami are hot. Those markets—and another dozen or so like them—have pushed home prices well into boom territory. It means there is a good chance you might be buying properties at inflated prices that, once the bubble burst, would come down again at lower prices. In markets like that, it is best to invest in apartments, but their prices also may be high.

Such large increases in home prices mean that demand for all housing is strong in these markets, both single-family and rentals. It is the local economy that drives demand for rentals, especially when many new jobs have only modest pay. Second, the local economies in these markets showed a significant increase in employment, better than the U.S. average.

Third, you want to study markets that, despite rising home prices, homes are not overpriced yet. You must choose an area showing a reasonable range of income so you are not buying into a boom that will eventually deflate.

It is an excellent time to invest in rentals. Research your markets, and you will improve your odds of success.

SUMMARY

I do hope your head is not spinning from explaining all the investment possibilities that you might consider. It would be best if you were considering one alternative for your first buy consideration—residential rentals. That being suggested, you have two choices, single-family rentals, and multi-family rentals (such as a duplex).

If your budget is tight, then the single-family owner-occupied investment would make the most sense. That is because you can buy with an FHA mortgage with only 3 ½ percent down. After a year of occupying it, you should plan to move out and lease it to a tenant to begin building your rental portfolio.

NEXT STEPS

The choice of location is important. Experienced investors know that you make your profit when you buy. To do this, you must make sure your investment is well located and at a price that will ensure your target profits in a future sale. The next chapter teaches you the importance of location and the techniques you can use to ensure that you have found the ideal neighborhood to lead to investment success.

CHAPTER FOUR

LOCUS, LOCUS, LOCUS

"If you don't own a home, buy one. If you own a home, buy another one. If you own two homes, buy a third."
　　　　　　　　　　　　　　　　　　　　—John Paulson

There is a hackneyed expression in real estate language that goes, "Location, location, location." I have heard it forever, which is why it is so annoying every time I hear it again. Even as I write it here, it makes me cringe a little. Yet, those that repeat it seem to feel that their audience has never heard of it. They do not realize that it has been around so long that even little children seem to know what it is referring to—and if you do not, bless you, bless you, and bless you.

Most of us know that it is a repeat of the oldest mantra in real estate, maybe even going back as far as Roman times where the forum crowd might be heard shouting, "Locus, locus, locus" (the Latin translation for location). The experienced can be forgiven, however, as what they are all trying to point out to the beginner is the ultra-importance of location when buying property.

As a new investor, the most important thing you can do to ensure your property's success is to locate it well. As part of that consideration, if you are investing in rentals, one thing to consider is that tenants should be in an area populated by tenants, not only homeowners. You want a mix, but you want tenants to predominate in the neighborhood. You will have a higher vacancy rate if you do not have a pool of potential tenants surrounding your property. Also, you must consider transportation issues such as nearness to downtown, bus stops, or train stations. Is it a convenient walk, or is it an Uber distance from civilization?

You Make Your Profit When You Buy

The choice of a location is important, as experienced investors know that you make your profit when you buy. Buying a property in a wanted location is part of the formula to assure profits. To make that profit when you buy, you must buy a property in an area in demand and at a price that will ensure your targeted profits in a future sale. If you overpay for a property, no amount of locating or improving it is going to make your investment pay off.

What Is a Good Income Property Location?

This chapter is all about finding the ideal location. You will use at least ten criteria to decide what areas are ideal property locations for rental investments. But knowing the ideal principles is just the start, as an investor must learn how to apply them. Here are the basics you should consider when analyzing a location:

- Good demand for rental units
- Nearness to public transportation
- Not an excess of rental properties
- Nearness to shopping, restaurants, and entertainment
- Low-crime area
- Airbnb is allowed
- Affordable real estate property prices
- Reasonable operating costs
- Area rental incomes provide positive cash flows
- Anticipated healthy future appreciation

THE IMPORTANCE OF PROPERTY LOCATION

Locations are fixed. An investment property will not have wheels (mobile homes being the exception), so if you find that your property's location is not ideal, you cannot just back up a truck and move it to a better site. In other words, you are stuck with its current location. Care must be taken to find the best location you can afford and one that brings cash flow.

Location desirability. Your location will decide your access to such things as utilities (gas, electricity, water, and the Internet). It will offer public transportation, schools and hospitals, shops and stores, cafes and restaurants, tourist attractions, and similar amenities. These attractions are essential to some groups and not especially relevant to others. For example, if you are choosing to rent to Airbnb clients, those tenants prefer intercity transportation, dining, and tourist areas. In contrast, traditional tenants look for good in-city transportation options, proximity to grocery stores, and excellent schools and hospitals. Both long-term tenants and Airbnb guests want a safe location with available and reliable utility supplies.

Supply and demand. Location is the determining factor for rental demand. It is obvious the higher the number of apartments and the lower the population, the higher the vacancy rate. You want an investment property with a balance between available rentals and the number of area tenants. We will show you how to figure that out in this chapter. It makes sense that you do not want to invest in areas with few tenants.

What Is a Good Income Property Location?

Good demand for rental units

Nearness to public transportation

Not an excess of rental properties

Low crime area

Airbnb is allowed

Affordable real estate property prices

Nearness to shopping, restaurants, and entertainment

RESTAURANT

airbnb

Reasonable operating costs

Area rental incomes provide positive cash flows

Anticipated healthy future appreciation

Figure 4. What makes a good income property location?

Rental strategy. The rental strategy is about how you will manage your rental investment. In today's marketplace, you have the choice of traditional renting or renting to Airbnb guests. Many landlords consider short-term rentals such as Airbnb too risky and far too much work. However, what a landlord might favor could be obviated by the profitability factor, as an Airbnb rental may produce a higher income than the monthly rent on a year-long lease. Airbnb is the most practical choice for certain locations, usually a more profitable business in an urban region because of transportation and entertainment factors. Then there are certain areas better for traditional rental units because of the neighborhood and its amenities. As a landlord, you would need to corroborate the legality of Airbnb in your community before opting for the Airbnb rental strategy.

Profitability. Rental income is based on supply and demand. The more vacant units, the lower the rents will be. The corollary is also true the lower the vacancy rate of an area, the higher the rents. The location also influences running costs such as taxes and utilities. These all impact your cash flow and profitability.

Appreciation. The location will decide the appreciation your property will or will not gain over time. Appreciation is usually attributed to demand. The higher the demand for an area, the greater the annual appreciation will be. Therefore, some neighborhoods appreciate more than others. Remember that as you evaluate locations.

HOW TO FIND THE BEST LOCATION

Finding the ideal location for your investment property depends on several criteria. You must consider the state, the city, town, village, the neighborhood, down to the street, and then which side of the street. You can choose the most vibrant city in the USA and then buy your property in the wrong neighborhood, and your income property will be at risk. Therefore, you must do some substantial analysis to decide the best state, city, and community to choose the right property.

To begin with, you are more likely to find a suitable property in a more expansive zip code. There are typically two and a half people in a home, so in a ten thousand-person zip code, you will find 4,000 properties (owner and rental). As previously mentioned, you increase your chance for long-term investment success by investing in areas with the highest concentration of renters.

For example, in Table2, below, 25 Best USA Rental Markets, was designed by Local Market Monitor. This company provides forecasts for house prices, rents, and investment risks. It is the data that you want to analyze to determine your best investment location. The reports are available at a cost on its website: localmarketmonitor.com. According to this data provider, these details are available for twenty thousand ZIP codes across the country. So, you should be able to find the exact data you need.

In examining the tables, take note of the movement of home prices versus rents. They both change in cycles but at different rates. Rents follow local earned income, whereas the cost of homes responds to relatively small changes in supply and demand. Your investment is less at risk in markets where home prices and rents increase slowly and steadily.

NEIGHBORHOOD FEATURES THAT INCREASE PROPERTY VALUE

The Coffee Effect. Between 1997 and 2014, homes within a quarter-mile of a Starbucks increased in value by 96 percent, on average, compared with 65 percent for all U.S. homes, based on a comparison of the Zillow Home Value Index data with a database of Starbucks locations.[1]

If you think all java purveyors have the same effect, the data showed that homes near Dunkin' Donuts locations appreciated 80 percent, on average, during the same 17-year period.

Urban versus suburban. The average urban home is now worth 35 percent more than the average suburban home. Since 2012, the median home value in urban areas has increased by 54 percent, while the median home value in suburban areas is up just 38 percent.[2]

Shopping. A research paper from the University of Chicago and Brigham Young University found homes close to grocery and shopping stores usually sell for more. Being close to a popular grocery store like Whole Foods has also shown to increase your home value, and having a 24-hour Walmart less than half a mile away has shown value increases of 2-3 percent.[3]

Trees. A survey from the University of Washington found that, on average, "trees in one's front yard add 3 to 5 percent to the home value, and in high-income areas, neighborhood trees can increase the area's value by up to 15 percent."[4]

Future amenities. News of a streetscaping plan in the works or new amenities planned for the area, or maybe desirable retailers coming to town, such as Trader Joe's, Whole Foods, or Target, further boost home values. [4]

Current amenities. Neighborhood amenities such as walkability, dog parks, and hiking trails increase home value in various amounts. [4]

NEIGHBORHOOD FEATURES THAT
DRAG DOWN PROPERTY VALUE

Landfills. When researchers looked at five municipal landfills near residential property in Cleveland, Ohio, they found the stench was enough to drag down property values by 5½ to 7⅓ percent. Landfills are most hurtful in populated, expensive, residential areas. The effect was nonexistent in sparse, rural areas. [4]

Power plants. The University of California at Berkeley has found that homes within 2 miles of power plants could be worth 3 to 7 percent less.[5]

Crime. Areas and neighborhoods with higher crime rates tend to see lower home values. The American Economic Review has found that if a registered sex offender were to move into your area, it could reduce your home's value by 12 percent.[6]

Low-rated schools. As we said above, top-rated schools are a big priority for some home buyers so homes located in areas with a low-ranking or closed school could result in a home value reduction of up to 22.2 percent.[7]

Cemeteries. Whether you believe in ghosts or not, living near a cemetery or funeral home is a bit eerie. According to Realtor.com, homes with a cemetery close by could be priced 12 percent less than homes in other nearby areas.[8]

Hospitals. You may think that being right around the corner from a hospital would be a good thing in the case of an emergency, but with hospitals come ambulances and sirens. And there is no telling what time of day or how many times a day you might hear these noises. Hospitals in nearness have decreased home values by around 3 percent.[9]

Shooting range. 3.7 percent
Funeral home. 6.5 percent
Homeless shelter. 12.7 percent
High renter concentration. 13.8 percent
Strip club. 14.7 percent

PRICE-TO-RENT RATIO

Examining the chart, 25 Best USA Rental Markets, note the right-hand column, titled Price-to-Rent Ratio. It is the ratio of home prices to annualized rent. Investors can use this ratio as a benchmark for estimating whether it is cheaper to rent or own property. As an example, say the average home price is listed at $250,000, and the average rent is $1,100 a month. The price-to-rent ratio formula is as follows:

Price-to-Rent Ratio = Home Price / (Monthly Rent x 12) Therefore, in this example, the price-to-rent ratio was calculated as:

$250,000 ÷ ($1,100 x 12)
$250,000 ÷ $24,000 = 18.9

HOW THE PRICE-TO-RENT RATIO WORKS

The ratio can guide you on whether a community's housing market is reasonably-priced or overpriced. Trulia.com also offers price-to-rent ratios on its website, titled "Trulia Rent Versus Buy Index." If you were following, you would have seen a rapid increase in this ratio before the housing crash of 2008-2009.

The higher the ratio, the less profitable the market will be for real estate investing. You should aim for 15 percent or less for a successful investment.

Homebuyers can use the ratio to decide if it is better to buy or rent in each area.

LOCATION'S ECONOMIC OVERVIEW

To properly analyze investment locations, you should understand the metropolitan statistical area (MSA). An MSA is a high-population-density geographic area with close economic ties throughout the region. An MSA is not legally incorporated as a city or town would be. It is also not a legal administrative division like a county or a separate entity like a state; thus, the precise definition of any given metropolitan area can vary with the source. A typical metropolitan area is centered on a single large city that carries large influence over the region.

Your investment location should be in an MSA or other population center with the best investment criteria possible. Later in your analysis, you will rate your property selection based on its neighborhood, school district, or street-level features.

What follows are the significant areas of analysis that you should consider when finding your best location.

25 Best USA Rental Markets

2018	Population	1-Year Home Price Change	Job Growth Rate	Price vs. Income Price	3-Year Population Growth	Average Home Price ($000)	Price to Rent Ratio
Colorado Springs, CO	697,856	12%	3.90%	9%	6%	292	21
Ogden, UT	642,850	11%	21%	16%	5%	267	24
Lakeland, FL	650,092	11%	2.50%	9%	8%	193	17
Stockton, CA	726,106	10%	3.40%	14%	4%	304	21
Fort Worth, TX	2,395,645	10%	2.80%	9%	6%	251	20
Nashville, TN	1,830,345	10%	2.20%	8%	6%	297	23
Jacksonville, FL	1,449,481	10%	3.20%	13%	6%	264	21
Orlando, FL	2,387,138	10%	3.80%	20%	8%	266	18
Charlotte, NC	2,426,363	9%	2.70%	3%	6%	279	23
Fresno, CA	974,861	9%	2.90%	0%	3%	244	21
Indianapolis, IN	1,988,817	9%	1.80%	-17%	3%	212	20
Atlanta, GA	5,710,795	9%	1.90%	5%	5%	250	18
Sacramento, CA	2,274,194	9%	1.80%	18%	4%	348	23
Grand Rapids, MI	1,038,583	9%	2.10%	6%	3%	198	23
Kansas City, MO	2,087,471	8%	2.10%	-3%	3%	209	19
McAllen, TX	842,304	8%	2.00%	0%	4%	159	18
Greenville, SC	874,869	8%	2.00%	1%	4%	233	22
Tucson, AZ	1,010,025	7%	1.80%	-5%	2%	219	20
Omaha, NE	915,312	7%	1.70%	-17%	3%	201	18
Minneapolis-St. Paul, MN	3,524,583	7%	1.90%	6%	3%	272	21
Raleigh, NC	1,273,568	6%	3.50%	-2%	7%	292	22
San Antonio, TX	2,384,075	6%	1.70%	5%	6%	242	20
Boston, MA	1,984,537	6%	2.20%	5%	3%	417	22
Winston-Salem, NC	659,330	6%	1.90%	-11%	2%	193	22
Oklahoma City, OK	1,358,452	6%	2.70%	4%	4%	192	19

Table 2. Best USA rental markets using price-to-rent ratio.

AREA ECONOMICS

Your real estate investment will only work if your tenant has a good and stable paying job. You would have a problem if your property were in a one-company town and the business moved out. Even if your tenant remained, community-wide rents would suffer, and vacancy rates would grow. To top it off, you would no longer sell your property for the value it had before the company moved.

Therefore, your first action is to understand the job market in the location that you are interested in. These are the questions you should tackle:

- Are jobs increasing or decreasing?
- What about worker incomes, are they increasing or decreasing?
- Review the area job distribution, including white-collar versus blue-collar jobs.
- Examine employer distribution. Is there a wide variety of employers, or is the number of employers limited?

Your objective is to find a location that offers a good employer and worker distribution. Salaries should be increasing, and unemployment should be low or falling.

You can research employment and learn about the local economy using the following sources:

The U.S. Bureau of Labor Statistics – The BLS provides many types of data for regions, states, and local areas. This federal agency tracks unemployment rates, statistics, and regional economic trends. You can find them at BLS.gov.

The area Chamber of Commerce – Most medium- to larger-sized towns have a Chamber of Commerce. It is operated by area businesses to promote the community's economics. An active Chamber of Commerce is a good sign of a thriving economy in an area. To find out more about its activities, search for it online.

The ten-year plan – Every ten years or so, a city or area will update its ten-year plan. By reviewing it, you will find useful information on population growth trends, building and expansion projects, and zoning and land planning. Visit the city hall or locate it by searching for it online.

Annual financial report – The local government creates this report as fiscal control and planning for tax purposes. A good community location is often tied to its finances. You can also search for this online.

AREA POPULATION STATUS

Jobs and population growth or decline are two important markers of an excellent rental investment location. Population increases when jobs are growing and, conversely, it declines as jobs disappear. Of course, it is not strictly employment that influences population movement. Added influences are property taxes, weather, housing availability, politics, and area amenities.

You should look for an increasing population as this creates a demand for real estate. The best of both worlds is higher demand combined with a limited supply. That translates into higher rents and prices for homes. That is how money is made in real estate investing.

In studying population growth, you want to narrow it down to a comparison between your metropolitan statistical area and one nearby. Further study is required for population growth in various communities within the MSA.

You may want to look at some added resources to study your area's population trends. These would include:

Census Bureau statistics. The U.S. Census Bureau can provide you population statistics. These demographics give you the capacity to evaluate population trends in your areas of interest.

Google search to find population data. Simply type in the location you are exploring and add the word population. Google will produce census data on the population.

Purchase a Local Market Monitor area report. It will provide several helpful statistics, including population. You can find it at localmarketmonitor.com.

THE PRICE-TO-RENT RATIO

As was pointed out earlier, the price-to-rent ratio is an excellent method to evaluate an area's potential profitability. The ratio is the median price of a house in an area divided by the median yearly rent.

Honolulu, San Francisco, and New York City are the cities with the highest price-to-rent ratios. That translates to buyer unfriendliness. San Francisco's ratio of 45 to 1 is the highest on the West Coast and probably the least favorable to investors. Runaway from that area—fast.

Swinging over to the East coast, we examine New York City (see table). Looking at New York City, one must drill down to find the price-to-rent ratio per borough as it varies. For example, if you examined the average city apartment renting for $12,000 a year, its cost should be $433,929. That ratio is for the city-wide market. That, however, represents the entire market in all five boroughs. In Manhattan and Brooklyn, the numbers look even worse. The table below lists the price-to-rent ratios for all five boroughs individually.

New York City Price to Rent Ratio Table

Location	Annual Rent	Sales Price	Price/Rent Ratio
City-Wide	$12,000	$433,929	36.16
Manhattan	$12,000	$599,760	49.98
Brooklyn	$12,000	$507,720	42.31
Queens	$12,000	$360,600	30.05
The Bronx	$12,000	$390,480	32.54
Staten Island	$12,000	$429,960	35.83

Table 3. New York City price-to-rent ratio table by borough.

None of New York City's price-to-rent ratios are attractive. So, it is best to look to other markets to invest.

HISTORICAL PRICE-TO-RENT RATIO

The state of the housing market rises and falls over the years, as do the national and city price-to-rent ratios. In the years before the housing bubble began, when the housing market heated up in 2005, the national rate rose from 22.73 in just two years to 24.50. But after the real estate market subsided beginning in 2007, home prices fell, and rentals became more expensive. The price-to-rent ratio started falling as well. By 2011 it had dropped down to the current rate of 18.92.

But before the housing bubble burst, the average price-to-rent ratio was reported about fifteen. So, the almost 19 to 1 ratio suggests that this period is more favorable to renters compared to the period before the housing crisis.

According to smartasset.com, as of April 22, 2020, San Francisco leads this list as the most attractive city in the U.S. for renters. It is not as attractive to homebuyers because of higher prices. The San Francisco median home value in 2018 was $1,195,700, and the median monthly rent was $1,880. That produces a price-to-rent ratio of 53.00. That would make a house bought for $500,000 (if you could find one) rent for $786.00 a month ($500,000 ÷ 53.00 = $9434).

Detroit, Michigan, has the lowest price-to-rent ratio across the country's 50 largest cities, meaning it is more favorable to homebuyers than renters. The 2018 median home value of a Detroit home was $51,600, and the 2018 median annual rent was $10,032, which produces a meager price-to-rent ratio of just 5.14. That would mean you could buy a property that would produce a monthly rent of $1000 for just $61,700.

From Zillow statistics as of March 2020, we can calculate the average U.S. price-to-rent ratio as 7.72 ($248,857 ÷ $19,224). As a guide, you want to make your rental investments between a 5 to 8 percent price-to-rent ratio for the best returns and cash flow.

However, the price-to-rent ratio is not the exclusive guide to use when choosing a location for your investment. If it were, then you would only purchase in Detroit and not in San Francisco.

This ratio is essential, but it is only a partial measure for location and must be combined with others. You must be a bit cynical of data, as a low price-to-rent ratio can at first seem significant. But you must ask yourself what may be the cause?

There are several excellent sources you can use that will provide current price-to-rent ratios. Zillow offers a local market report using national sales and rent data. Local Market Monitor should be consulted as they have excellent data. The local MLS can also be tapped to give you the most current rent and price information in your area of interest.

THE HOW MUCH TO PAY TABLE

There is another helpful report you can access at Local Market Monitor. Two different markets are shown here with permission from the *Local Market Monitor*. They are the Indianapolis, Indiana, and Newark, New Jersey reports. We included these so you could see the differences in two diverse locations.

The reports provide some location information, which will be helpful to anyone conducting location research. They have not only the population of each community but also the single-family home price range and the percent of renters. Also, the average monthly rent is included, with three years of home price appreciation. These are important numbers in your location search and go a long way to lessening the time looking up individual data. It is all here in one table.

It is interesting to take some time to compare both location tables. You will see how diverse locations can be. They show potential attractive communities (remember you need eyes on the ground in the end) as well as communities you should stay away from as either being too expensive or not having a large enough renter population.

HOW MUCH TO PAY
The Price Guide for Local Zip Codes

Indianapolis-Carmel
Indiana

Zip Code		Pop.	Renters	Favored Price Range		Average Rent 2020	Rent Forecast 3 Years	Home Price Increase 2017	2018	Estimate 2019
46001	ALEXANDRIA IN	10,185	24%	179,300	248,300	$810	2%	10%	3%	5%
46011	ANDERSON IN	17,021	21%	174,200	335,000	$943	2%	10%	1%	4%
46012	ANDERSON IN	19,306	32%	171,100	263,300	$849	2%	3%	7%	6%
46013	ANDERSON IN	17,330	34%	177,800	246,200	$819	3%	7%	7%	6%
46016	ANDERSON IN	18,300	57%	142,900	195,600	$741	2%	4%	0%	3%
46017	ANDERSON IN	5,736	21%	155,100	209,800	$795	3%	2%	10%	7%
46032	CARMEL IN	47,108	32%	267,500	352,000	$1,275	11%	9%	5%	9%
46033	CARMEL IN	38,275	9%	278,700	355,500	$1,347	10%	4%	5%	8%
46034	CICERO IN	6,845	15%	174,400	226,100	$857	12%	5%	9%	9%
46036	ELWOOD IN	11,756	31%	155,900	255,100	$787	2%	5%	4%	4%
46037	FISHERS IN	40,798	15%	293,600	559,300	$1,432	11%	2%	8%	8%
46038	FISHERS IN	42,003	27%	262,800	343,100	$1,300	12%	5%	8%	9%
46040	FORTVILLE IN	11,525	16%	243,400	251,600	$953	18%	-2%	14%	11%
46052	LEBANON IN	21,969	30%	174,900	229,700	$870	13%	4%	3%	8%
46055	MC CORDSVILLE IN	11,445	7%	251,700	364,300	$1,245	15%	2%	6%	8%
46060	NOBLESVILLE IN	39,986	30%	262,500	345,400	$1,163	12%	7%	7%	9%
46062	NOBLESVILLE IN	34,420	20%	207,500	275,300	$1,043	10%	10%	2%	7%
46064	PENDLETON IN	16,856	20%	167,900	322,900	$981	2%	10%	3%	5%
46069	SHERIDAN IN	7,600	27%	172,400	238,700	$860	11%	8%	4%	8%
46072	TIPTON IN	9,084	25%	157,500	257,800	$832	17%	8%	0%	6%
46074	WESTFIELD IN	31,580	19%	246,500	435,000	$1,247	13%	11%	8%	10%
46077	ZIONSVILLE IN	27,666	16%	254,700	469,200	$1,397	17%	6%	10%	11%
46106	BARGERSVILLE IN	6,008	25%	186,700	333,200	$1,112	16%	4%	5%	7%
46107	BEECH GROVE IN	12,644	41%	175,200	242,600	$867	16%	18%	6%	8%
46112	BROWNSBURG IN	36,213	20%	206,100	377,900	$1,187	13%	5%	8%	10%
46113	CAMBY IN	15,663	20%	211,000	351,700	$1,162	16%	9%	10%	8%
46118	CLAYTON IN	5,196	19%	276,600	329,200	$1,101	10%	7%	0%	7%
46120	CLOVERDALE IN	5,319	23%	214,600	229,000	$788	7%	4%	-1%	3%
46121	COATESVILLE IN	5,291	10%	167,800	203,200	$770	10%	6%	8%	7%
46122	DANVILLE IN	15,963	26%	165,100	335,000	$983	13%	4%	8%	9%

THE EXPERTS IN LOCAL MARKETS

Table 4. How much to pay in Indiana with permission of Local Market Monitor.

HOW MUCH TO PAY
The Price Guide for Local Zip Codes

Newark
New Jersey

Zip Code		Pop.	Renters	Favored Price Range		Average Rent 2020	Rent Forecast 3 Years	Home Price Increase 2017	2018	Estimate 2019
07003	BLOOMFIELD NJ	48,892	47%	286,400	477,400	$1,464	15%	5%	5%	5%
07004	FAIRFIELD NJ	7,584	8%	432,200	598,400	$2,149	16%	4%	7%	5%
07005	BOONTON NJ	15,350	22%	279,100	531,700	$1,511	7%	4%	4%	4%
07006	CALDWELL NJ	25,712	24%	388,900	541,200	$1,604	12%	5%	1%	3%
07009	CEDAR GROVE NJ	12,638	21%	362,600	552,600	$1,574	13%	6%	2%	3%
07016	CRANFORD NJ	23,972	22%	459,300	636,000	$1,778	10%	3%	3%	4%
07017	EAST ORANGE NJ	36,304	71%	220,200	356,300	$1,134	21%	3%	16%	9%
07018	EAST ORANGE NJ	28,922	77%	268,800	352,000	$1,216	6%	8%	-11%	-2%
07023	FANWOOD NJ	7,648	12%	694,000	793,100	$3,077	10%	1%	5%	4%
07028	GLEN RIDGE NJ	7,791	8%	376,700	524,100	$1,675	16%	4%	8%	6%
07033	KENILWORTH NJ	8,235	22%	323,900	551,400	$1,614	10%	3%	4%	4%
07034	LAKE HIAWATHA NJ	9,308	35%	276,300	360,100	$1,364	7%	6%	2%	3%
07035	LINCOLN PARK NJ	10,707	23%	446,700	549,800	$1,798	7%	6%	0%	2%
07036	LINDEN NJ	43,727	43%	283,200	472,000	$1,364	12%	2%	9%	6%
07039	LIVINGSTON NJ	29,955	11%	639,700	942,800	$2,949	13%	5%	2%	3%
07040	MAPLEWOOD NJ	24,543	23%	375,500	522,500	$1,670	14%	6%	3%	4%
07041	MILLBURN NJ	7,283	36%	380,100	528,800	$1,859	13%	2%	4%	3%
07042	MONTCLAIR NJ	26,323	51%	374,700	521,300	$1,680	15%	7%	5%	5%
07043	MONTCLAIR NJ	12,689	20%	362,300	504,100	$1,952	13%	5%	2%	4%
07044	VERONA NJ	13,893	19%	355,000	473,400	$1,608	13%	5%	2%	3%
07045	MONTVILLE NJ	10,732	7%	527,800	985,200	$2,561	6%	2%	1%	2%
07050	ORANGE NJ	30,644	77%	254,900	335,400	$1,206	19%	21%	5%	8%
07052	WEST ORANGE NJ	47,609	33%	385,200	536,000	$1,633	15%	5%	6%	5%
07054	PARSIPPANY NJ	29,889	48%	296,500	375,800	$1,424	8%	4%	4%	4%
07058	PINE BROOK NJ	5,004	52%	451,300	555,500	$1,801	8%	7%	5%	5%
07059	WARREN NJ	15,982	8%	295,500	652,600	$1,759	10%	-1%	8%	4%
07060	PLAINFIELD NJ	46,270	60%	259,500	478,100	$1,358	13%	5%	10%	8%
07062	PLAINFIELD NJ	12,793	39%	301,600	430,900	$1,430	12%	7%	6%	6%
07063	PLAINFIELD NJ	14,031	33%	319,800	544,300	$1,556	17%	0%	21%	11%
07065	RAHWAY NJ	29,471	41%	458,000	563,700	$1,606	13%	9%	8%	7%

THE EXPERTS IN LOCAL MARKETS

Table 5. How much to pay in Northern New Jersey with permission of Local Market Monitor.

Your Location Criteria

A location that has the most robust demand should be part of your needs. It can be found by analyzing the distribution rents in each ZIP code, which can be quite different from one community to another. This range changes from year to year, so you must look at current information.

Some markets with large renter populations are better investment bets, even though demand will flatten everywhere for a short while. Also, though these markets do not show high growth rates, importantly, they are not over-priced. Also, the ratio of home prices to annual rents is favorable. Look at Chicago, Memphis, Detroit, and Atlanta.

According to Ingo Winzer, writing for Forbes, "Because there hasn't been enough home construction in the past decade—and much of that construction has been of higher-priced homes—there is already unmet demand for rentals; that demand will increase for years no matter what happens right now. Investors do not need to rush, looking for bargains. They can take their time to find the markets that will best suit their financial goals."[12]

Note the home-price-to-rent ratio in most of these markets is 21 or less. It means single-family homes can be bought and rented out with small extra expense. You will be better-off cutting single-family homes into several rental units in higher-ratio markets like Milwaukee and Madison. The low-ratio markets like Peoria, Rockford, Champaign-Urbana, and Wichita offer some speculative bargain opportunities.

Whether you plan for long-term investments, flip properties, or upgrade to higher rents, your investment strategy improves if you know the favored price range and the current average rent rate in a community. That is where the most substantial demand is. Below the preferred price range, you have more credit risk from your renters; above the range, you have a smaller number of renters. Both can be big problems when the local economy slows.

HOW LOCATION AFFECTS HOME VALUE

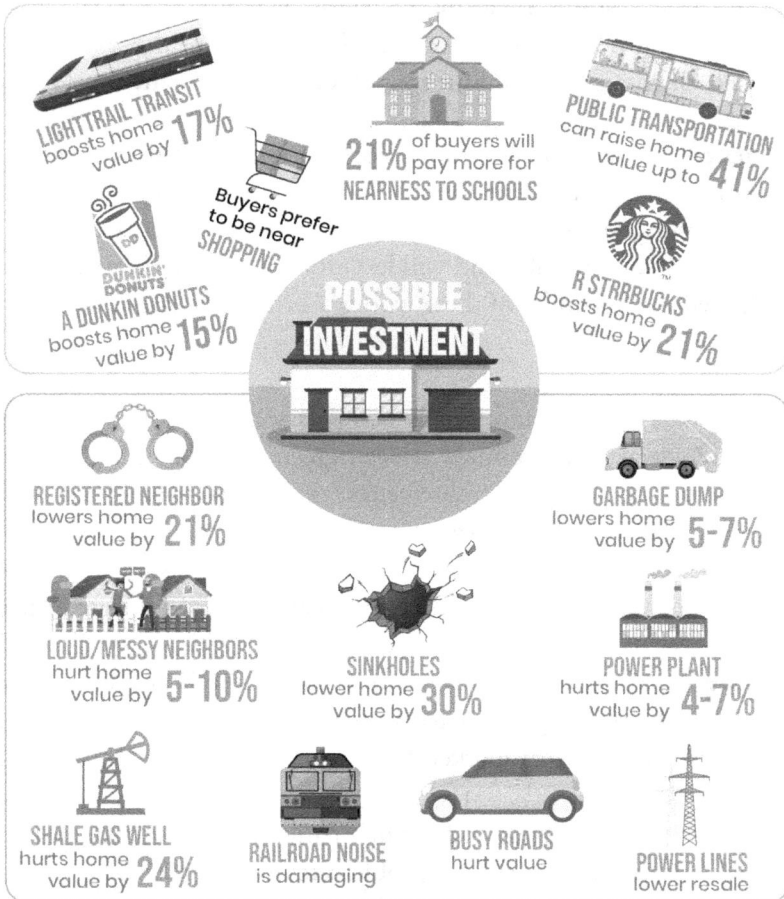

LIGHT TRAIL TRANSIT boosts home value by **17%**

Buyers prefer to be near SHOPPING

A DUNKIN DONUTS boosts home value by **15%**

21% of buyers will pay more for NEARNESS TO SCHOOLS

PUBLIC TRANSPORTATION can raise home value up to **41%**

R STRRBUCKS boosts home value by **21%**

POSSIBLE INVESTMENT

REGISTERED NEIGHBOR lowers home value by **21%**

GARBAGE DUMP lowers home value by **5-7%**

LOUD/MESSY NEIGHBORS hurt home value by **5-10%**

SINKHOLES lower home value by **30%**

POWER PLANT hurts home value by **4-7%**

SHALE GAS WELL hurts home value by **24%**

RAILROAD NOISE is damaging

BUSY ROADS hurt value

POWER LINES lower resale

Figure 5. How location affects market value.

The average monthly rent is the minimum you should be after.

The good news is that all this analysis is done for you by a company called Local Market Monitor located in Cary, North Carolina. According to its website, the company provides national real estate economic analysis and forecasting tools, offering investors in properties and home mortgages the local market risk intelligence they need to make informed decisions.

You can buy its helpful reports from its website; page samples are included here. You can judge its value. However, it makes it easy to locate the renters and learn the average rents to help estimate the value of your next rental purchase.

Real estate location is about local analysis, as housing and rental demand vary from neighborhood to neighborhood. Let us examine those characteristics that make each community unique for real estate investment consideration.

Convenience. A good rule of thumb for real estate investment is no more distant from a major economic center than ten miles. Most tenants want to live near shopping, schools, and, of course, their jobs. Fewer people will want to travel more than ten miles and will look for the most convenient location. By keeping within ten miles of these, you will attract the largest percentage of the population.

Attraction. This is what emotionally compels someone to an area or place. It would include parks, tree-lined streets, green spaces, charming shopping districts, coffee shops and microbreweries, mountains, water, rivers, and so on. Since attractions vary by location, you must get out and walk the street yourself to get the feel of the neighborhoods. Google's instantstreetview.com will not do it for you. Nothing beats an in-person visit for accurate inspection.

Walk rating. This is an essential factor for renters. Zillow's research found that better nearness by walking correlated to higher property appreciation as well as better price resilience in a market downturn.

Safety & crime rates. Buyers and tenants nationwide want safe areas to live in. Areas of higher crime are also a problem for property owners, who suffer theft and property damage and drugs. You are better off to abandon a good deal if you discover it is a neighborhood with high crime rates.

You can research safety and crime rates using City-data.com's crime reports. ADT offers a crime map, and you can use Trulia.com to find these details by searching its map feature. Finally, make sure you visit the neighborhood and eyeball it yourself.

School districts. You will want to check out school districts in the location you are examining. The quality of the school is high on the list of importance for renters and buyers. An excellent place to start is a website called Greatschools.com, which rates schools for you. You can also question residents as well as real estate agents for their recommendations.

Public transportation. Public transportation is especially important in urban areas. A property located near bus routes and trains is a highly prized amenity. You can research this through the local transit system's website or use Google Transit, which uses Google Maps to provide transit maps around the world. Locate the bus stops and railway stations near the property you are exploring.

The HOA and neighborhood covenants. If your property is in a neighborhood with covenants and restrictions, you must be sure you fully understand them. Some HOAs forbid renting, and you should be aware of this in advance. HOAs require fees that can vary significantly. You want to avoid properties with high fees and strict covenants.

Local laws, finances, taxes, and infrastructure. You must pay attention to local laws and restrictive fees. Carefully examine property taxes and their past trends. What are the municipal services such as trash pickup, and are they included in property taxes? Examine local municipal services and planning codes.

Many communities throughout the country have rent control rules. Make certain you check this out. Do you need a certificate of occupancy? Is there a fee due for tenant rentals? Must there be a vacant apartment inspection? What about smoke detector regulations? All these issues need time and money and should impact your buying decisions.

You should also become familiar with the local eviction laws, laws vary widely. Are they tenant-friendly, or are they landlord-friendly?

You can usually find all the answers on the municipalities' websites or at the local code enforcement office in town.

MORE UNEXPECTED MARKETS

According to Ingo Wizer, president of Local Market Monitor, writing for Forbes, "Investors must think beyond areas such as San Francisco and Seattle. Cities like Orlando, Phoenix, Charlotte, Charleston, and almost anywhere in Texas are all projected to see dramatic spikes in home values as more people move there in search of jobs and good places to raise families. While it can be hard to predict just what market will explode in the years to come (how many times have you heard an investment company tell you that their city is 'the next Seattle'), it can help to look at a variety of factors. These would include— population growth, job markets, and rental rates are all essential pieces of the puzzle. Some investors are also holding out hope that markets in the 2008 housing crash will begin to pick up in 2020."[12]

But an investor must be careful, as there are still pockets of unemployment in these cities. Some places might have a single large employer such as a military base. You must weigh these factors when you consider an area to invest in.

SUMMARY

We hope we impressed on you the key to success is to ensure your new investment is well located. To help you find suitable locations, we supplied you with a significant number of sources that you can research. Many websites such as Trulia and Zillow have excellent information to zero in on great renter-friendly communities.

We also went over the price-to-rent ratio and showed you how to apply it as an investor and as a house buyer. As an investor, we recommended you stay under a ratio of 15 in each area you are considering. With the lower ratio being renter-friendly and the higher ratio being homeowner-friendly.

Also, when researching locations, you must make in-person visits to the neighborhoods you are considering. It will enable you to question neighbors and local real estate brokers. Person-to-person contacts are a critical ingredient of your information gathering.

NEXT STEPS

Now that you have learned how to find the best locations, the critical step is understanding how to find that good deal. There are many ways that investors can find rental properties to invest in. The next chapter provides you the techniques that give you the highest chance of finding the best investment fit and the right deal for you. As you read through it, you will find that it leads you through the methods used experienced by investors to find those deals and make that excellent investment.

CHAPTER FIVE

HOW TO FIND THE DEALS

*"Buying real estate is not only the best way, the quickest way,
the safest way, but the only way to become wealthy."*
—Marshall Field, entrepreneur

I n June of 1983, a group of friends and I had the exhilarating experience of rafting the Snowy River. It was perfect weather and, indeed, a memorable adventure. The Snowy Gorge is especially exciting with its powerful rapids and amazing sheer 600-foot-high cliffs.

As we came to our first rapids, the water was accelerating between the rocks, carrying us down to the next level, where we had to turn quickly to line up for the next chute. If we missed it, we would surely be stranded on the rocks and find ourselves at the mercy of the rapidly flowing current.

Just as we eased our way into the narrow chute and congratulated ourselves on our skillful maneuvering, our guide yelled out, "Paddle, Paddle, Paddle! Do it! Hard!"

Startled at our guide's surprise instructions, we paddled as furiously as we could, speeding up through the chute before we took a sharp right turn to line up to enter the next set of rapids.

Relieved and soaked to the skin, we let out a cheer as we shot into the current until our guide silenced us by raising his voice over the roar of the water. "You know why we had to paddle so hard just when the current was carrying us at our fastest?" We did not. "It's because, no matter how fast the current, you have to be going faster if you want to have any say in where you go next."

That story could not be more appropriate for what you must do next. You must move quicker than others who will also be searching for the same deals. You see, if there is an issue that can be more discouraging than losing a deal, it is locating good real estate deals. Since we are suggesting that you perform this feat in ninety days, we better have a way of helping you through the maze of real estate rapids and currents that you will surely face.

At first, as we did on that raft, you will struggle with this as it is so new. However, we have designed this chapter to take you by the hand and lead you through it. Let me start by reassuring you there are multiple ways to find deals that will provide you the cash flow you are aiming for. But, the good ones do not fall in your lap, as you must paddle hard to reach them. You have to develop a competitive advantage as you work to find them.

THE MULTIPLE LISTING SERVICE

Start with the Multiple Listing Service in your community. The MLS website is the number one site to use for your search as it contains the most valuable information. The Multiple Listing Service (MLS) is a business association formed by groups of real estate brokers throughout the country. They band together to create an online database exclusive to members of the National Real Estate Association, which allows them to see one another's listings of properties for sale. There can even be several MLS areas covering the same area. Unfortunately, public access to its online services is limited, often only showing what properties are for sale. Member brokers, however, can also see prices of closed sales and what properties were listed but were withdrawn.[1]

OTHER PROPERTY LISTING WEBSITES

You can also find the properties for sale on Realtor.com if you cannot access the MLS in your area. While both the MLS and public listing sites such as Realtor.com may feature some of the same listings, they differ. MLS information is more comprehensive. But Realtor.com is a free site that provides you the phone number of each broker of property in each area. You can collect those numbers and reach out to the agents to gather information on leads. However, the site does not show what properties have sold.

Check out the ZipRealty.com website. It also includes the property price but goes one step further, including price changes and whether the property is a short sale or REO. It is valuable information when negotiations begin. Another website, Trulia.com, offers users market trend analyses, neighborhood comparisons, and the capacity to search through various categories of listings, such as foreclosures, resales, or for sale by owner properties. Another valuable property research website is Zillow.com. It is like Trulia and provides accurate home value estimates for every property. It also lists sold comps.

If you are in a major population area, Redfin.com will provide better information. This site is a free way to get access to closed comps that MLS would offer you. However, if you are not located within Redfin's working areas, then you can try the less used, but amazingly effective MLS plan BA (broker's assistant) method.

As a final note, with Realtor.com and Zillow.com, once a house goes pending or is closed, you can no longer see a photo of the house. The only place a photo exists of a sold home is on the local MLS. You do not know how many days the property was on the market before it sold or how many price decreases were made.

THE BROKER'S ASSISTANT METHOD

The broker's assistant method takes a bit more finesse to carry out. But it can be unbelievably valuable. An investor-friendly agent can grant a person MLS access by setting them up as an unlicensed assistant at their brokerage firm.

To achieve this method, you need to polish your negotiation skills. That is because you will need to convince an agent to form a partnership with you. It can be done by offering them a flat fee, finder's percentage fee, or a combination of both. You will also need to explain how the arrangement will benefit the broker's business. You can locate an investor-friendly agent through advertisements on Craigslist or LinkedIn. You can also place an active advertisement on Facebook groups, agent forums, or your real estate network.

By getting access to the full MLS, you will have access to the expired and withdrawn sales. It lets you see which properties fell apart on the market and which did not sell.

TEAM UP WITH AN INVESTMENT-SAVVY REAL ESTATE BROKER

The next step in your goal to buy your first real estate investment property is to find a real estate broker specializing in investment properties—even better, one that owns some as well. Locating a real estate broker that is investment property oriented is an unbelievably valuable resource. That does not cost you a thing as the seller pays the broker. Have your agent set you up to automatically email you listings based on the criteria and locations you have established. One of the services your agent might perform for you is to set up his MLS to email you a customized search. It is the sign of a valuable agent as not all will set up a search for you other than active listings. Therefore, you will have to specify any added needed information such as price decreases, pending sales, or sold sales data. You can request the listings be limited to specific areas down to a subdivision or even a street.

Another significant advantage of working with an investment-oriented broker is the agent will know potential investment properties even before they go on the MLS. It will give you a great competitive paddling advantage. Any time a property comes on the market, you will be instantly notified.

DRIVING FOR DOLLARS

Driving for dollars is a term that real estate investors use to describe a technique for finding great deals on houses. You drive through various neighborhoods until you find a property that looks vacant or distressed. Homes that are not maintained show the owner does not care about the house, is short on money, or has given up. Write down the addresses of all the properties that you are interested in. Then when you return home, you look up the owner's name and contact information. It is not easy to find the owner. You must search at the town or county records offices. But when you have determined who the owner is, you contact them and try to buy the property. If the house is bank-owned, it is challenging to buy it from them as they now use specified real estate agents for these sales.

Driving around and spotting potential houses that might be ready for sale is simple, but finding owners and buying the home can be complicated. But the reward can be significant.

DIRECT MAIL MARKETING TECHNIQUE

Direct mail can be an effective method of finding great deals. The first step in this approach is to set up a high-quality source of property ownership data. You can find this from title companies as they have the most accurate data based on hundreds of years of parcel transaction history. It is all documented and well organized.

Next, you want to narrow down the list to find properties the owner no longer wants. These are the ones that are owned by out-of-state owners, have piled up back taxes, and have no mortgage debt, which makes for high return buys. According to a 2019 report by Forbes, about forty percent of property owners have no mortgage associated with their homes.[2] Because of these issues, the owners are motivated to sell it to you for any price you offer.

Here is a list of direct mail companies specializing in developing real estate leads:

- offers2owners.com
- click2mail.com
- yellowletterservice.com
- letterprinting.net
- letterstream.com

Step three is to send an offer. You do not need to send a letter inquiring if the owner wishes to sell. Because you have reviewed the data before, there is no doubt about it. So, do not waste time. Just send the offer. The chances are high the owners are willing to accept it for much less than the property is worth.

After your offer is received, you will be besieged by signed agreements as well as telephone calls. You now want to do your property inspection in anticipation of a purchase. It is just the opposite of the traditional method of first looking and then offering. It is a time-saver.

The final step is to call your attorney or escrow agent to let them close the deal.

HOW TO START WITH NO CASH

Dedicate yourself to learning how to find great real estate deals. If you do not have money, you can begin by flipping real estate deals with wholesalers. You can find them on Craigslist in your area. As an example, here is a suggested advertisement you might try:

"I'm new in real estate and incredibly good at finding off-market, underpriced, undervalued houses in the X area. I am buying a property for about 40% under market value and do not have the money to close the deal. I do not want this deal to go to waste. Give me a call if you would like to complete the transaction together. There is $50,000 of margin in the sale, and I will take $15K. I have several others on the way from many direct mail campaigns."

WHOLESALING – THE MIDDLEMAN

In real estate wholesaling, the wholesaler obtains a purchase contract for a seller's property. The wholesaler then finds another buyer for the property at a higher price. The wholesaler keeps the difference as profit like a finder's fee, but with some added documents thrown in. Real estate wholesalers find and contract distressed properties.

Wholesaling can be done with minimal funds, which makes it a starting point for new investors with little starting capital. Wholesaling is more about marketing and less about investing, as the best wholesalers are the best marketers. Though this may sound like an excellent place for a beginner to find deals of forty percent below market, it needs great skill that even experienced investors give up on. It is tough work. You must be willing to do what no one else will do—hustle.

REAL ESTATE AUCTIONS

Auctions are a good source of undervalued real estate. They are sold to the public through competitive bidding. Bidding is either done online through several auction sites or in person at the courthouse steps. All types of properties are available, including fixer-uppers, flips, and long-term holds.

The process is swift. You must place a five-to-ten-percent cash (cashier's check) deposit. You bid on the date announced, and if you are the high bidder, payment is due within thirty to forty-five days.

Properties that are auctioned are there because the owners were behind on their loan payments. That often means the properties may not have been kept up. Auction homes provide a few benefits, but many of the houses do not qualify for a mortgage.

A significant difference between buying a home at auction and the traditional route is that you do not get to go inside the house before putting in an offer. Many homes are bank-owned and in foreclosure. The other big issue is that you cannot get a mortgage or use a lender, as real estate auctions are all about cash. Buying a foreclosure "as is" means you could end with a bad roof, a basement full of water, or no bathroom fixtures.

Leading real estate auction websites include:

- RealtyTrac.com
- Auction.com
- Foreclosure.com
- RealtyBid.com
- Hubzu.com
- Bid4Asset.com

ESTABLISH A LEAD GENERATING WEBSITE

Establish a lead producing website with lead landing pages. The idea is to use Facebook advertising to push potential leads to the site, and then once they are on the site, use specific, landing pages to create leads.

Landing pages should be:

- Clean and clutter-free

- Have an easily seen "call to action"
- Contain exciting videos and images
- Use a lead inquiry form

Considering using landing pages with:

- Testimonials
- A lead magnet

The landing page should avoid:

- Your image
- Your company bio
- Multiple messages
- Navigation buttons
- Overly spammy, *salesy*, or wordy text

For an excellent example of a lead-generating website, see webuy-houses.com.

Utilizing a company like Home Value or leadpropeller.com can help real estate sites to excel at lead production. But each requires a monthly fee. If your budget is a consideration, you might try a do-it-yourself website from wix.com or godaddy.com.

GREAT REAL ESTATE LEADS FROM CRAIGSLIST ADVERTISEMENTS

Craigslist has been a lead generator for investors since its inception.

The website allows for the free posting of nearly anything. But to get real estate leads from Craigslist, one needs to follow a system for publishing advertisements. You first need to choose the kinds of leads that you are looking for. Here are the more specific subjects: foreclosure buyers, lease option buyers, apartment building buyers, luxury home buyers, first-time home buyers, buyers in a school district, and the like.

If you post an advertisement in one city, you might receive a few responses, and if you post it in many cities, you will get answers daily. This method does not cost you a cent. While you are on Craigslist, look at deals that are listed for sale that might work for you.

Craigslist ads disappear very quickly as newer advertisements are posted. Thus, you need to re-post them frequently. But, as a caution, you cannot re-post them too often, or they will be interpreted as spam and your advertisement will be taken down.

The timing of your posting can be critical, too, as research shows that Craigslist is most visited in the mornings between 8:30 and 9:00 am. It is just before work. It is recommended that you post twice daily during the week and at least once a day on the weekends. If you do not post, you will not get leads, so make sure you stay consistent.

TRADITIONAL NEWSPAPER ADVERTISEMENTS STILL WORK

Newspapers no longer have the readers they once had. Now, many more neighborhoods and communities have newspapers with limited circulation, and they will often sell newspaper advertisement space to help offset publication costs. This usually produces better results than a city-wide paper because it is targeted to a specific niche. If your local newsletters and weekly magazines have large classified sections, you should consider advertising with them. Look for where your competitors are advertising. If you do not see them in a classified section, then it may not be worth the cost to advertise with the paper. To be successful, your media should always contain an extensive classified section.

A well-written classified advertisement seeking owners wishing to sell a piece of real estate can attract interest from potential sellers or curious investors. You want to craft the right language and information to motivate people to contact you about their property. Owners and investors, and those who are looking for a buyer for a house or some land, are the audiences you are writing for.

Write a classified real estate advertisement that includes descriptive information, attention-grabbing language, and contact information. Your audience will see many advertisements, so you want a headline that will stand out. When designing your newspaper advertisement, make sure you are consistent with the rest of your marketing aesthetic. Link the advertisement to your website where visitors can learn more about you and your purchasing methods.

Also, do not forget to scan the local newspaper daily to check for sale by owner advertisements (FSBO) that may lead to a good deal.

ONLINE ADVERTISEMENTS

Realtors have been using Facebook to pull listing traffic and leads, and so should you. Your website can drive traffic using only a single method, whereas Facebook offers at least four ways. Here they are.

Viral sharing. Facebook provides you with free viral advertising. It only requires that you post exciting advertisements, offers, and tidbits on your Facebook page. So that anytime a reader Likes, comments, or shares one of your wall posts, it is also visible to the friends of that person. Since each person has an average of three hundred friends on Facebook, the free viral marketing of your Facebook Page can explode with action. Here are a few posts that appear on Facebook when you type in "I Buy Houses":

> *I have a few off-market deals in Philadelphia looking for cash buyers. DM me for details.*

> *We buy your house.*
> *Any house, ?*
> *Any condition. ?*
> *We see it, we like it, we buy it ?*
> *Fast cash…*

> *Are you in dire need of a loan? Has the bank refused to offer you their loan? Is your credit score poor? Or you do not have a collateral to obtain a loan? I can help you with a loan at a 5% interest rate. If you want to secure 100% legitimate funding, please get back to me so we can begin your loan processing.*
> *Do you need to sell your house fast? We want to buy your home no matter the condition. Call or text your address for a fast no-obligation offer. Call or Text …*

You might post an advertisement something like this to get the maximum response:

ANY PRICE, ANY LOCATION, ANY SITUATION!!
FAST CLOSING OR YOU CHOSE CLOSING DATE!!!

Posting on high-traffic walls. Another excellent way to get free leads on Facebook is by posting on high-traffic Fan Pages in your local market. Established Fan Pages will have many more followers than your Page. By posting on these Fan Pages, you are generating free exposure and marketing for your Page.

Facebook sidebar advertisements. The next two methods require a payment. It may be well worth it as it is all done automatically for you—there is no need to post anything except for the initial advertisement

The Facebook sidebar advertisement is the first recommended method. Sidebar advertisements appear on the side of the Facebook site.

It is an excellent method for getting likes and followers. But it is often misused, and the results are wasted. If you set it up wrongly, you will waste your money.

Use promoted posts on Facebook. The Facebook promoted post is probably the best-paid advertising method available for lead generation. A promoted post is a wall post that shows up in other peoples' news feeds. You can tell Facebook precisely who you want to show your advertisement to and in what geographical location. Facebook promoted posts have a limit in that they are only available to pages with more than four hundred *Likes*. Also, you can only run a promotion on posts that are newer than three days old. Finally, "fun" posts get over twice as many clicks as "salesy" posts. Not surprising that a fun post is going to get more engagement.

PRINT ADVERTISEMENTS – "WE BUY HOUSES"

With a bit larger budget, print is an excellent alternative to get property seller leads. As an example, your printed fliers can be attached to car windshields in parking lots. Then there are the "We Buy Houses" signs. You see them on telephone poles around town. You may have wondered, do homeowners sell their homes by calling the phone numbers on these signs? Most importantly, is there an opportunity for real estate investors here? They are often used by wholesalers, who find motivated sellers desperate to sell their homes in as-is condition and sell them to investors who buy, renovate, and resell to retail buyers. Wholesalers do not buy these homes. They contract with a seller and flip the contract to a buyer, making a profit on the transaction.

WORD-OF-MOUTH LEAD GENERATION

Word-of-mouth lead generation is gaining leads via one person speaking to another about your real estate agent services. There is nothing like passion for creating word of mouth. The more you talk about your business to friends and strangers, the more opportunity you develop for receiving leads. Ask your friends, family, and clients to spread the word. Ask for testimonials, put them on your website, and share them on your social networks such as Facebook. You can urge your contacts to go into Yelp, Google Business, or Facebook and leave a review of your wish to buy real estate properties. Once positive testimonials are on these platforms, they can stay there forever.

Will all these lead producing methods work for you? The answer is no. That is why we have listed so many for you to choose from. Every area of the country is different, much as suburban regions are different from cities. With all the choices we have provided, you will find two or three of your favorite ways of getting actionable leads.

We suggest you begin with the traditional standby—your local multiple listing service—as well as a local broker who owns investment properties themselves. Those two go-to sources should be all you need for your first investment. But you can certainly experiment with the others we have named here.

FINDING AN INVESTOR-FRIENDLY REAL ESTATE BROKER

Every investor needs an investor-friendly real estate agent with an excellent real estate investment broker as a part of their team. As an investor, you will need a real estate agent investor on your side who knows what you are looking for.

Most real estate agents have no idea about real estate investing. They are used to working with homeowners who want to live in a house as their primary residence. The homeowners are not looking for the best deal or cash flow. They are not thinking about flipping a home either. They want something that will be nice for their family and maybe a decent deal and plans to live there for years. As an investor, you have many different priorities. If you are investing for cash flow, you will want to know what it rents for and all the costs involved. If the target is to flip it, you will need to know what it will sell for after it is renovated and how much the repairs will cost. What most real estate brokers do not understand is that a good deal for a home buyer might be five to ten percent below market value. To an investor, a good deal would be twenty to thirty percent or more below market value. As a result, most real estate brokers do not realize how good of a deal an investor needs to make it work.

So, you cannot rely on a real estate agent to tell you what a good deal a property is. You need to know that yourself. You need to know the numbers and what criteria you are looking for. Most real estate agents do not invest in rental properties. They do not invest in fix-and-flips. Remember that their primary goal is to sell houses, not investments.

The biggest mistake that investors make is that they use an agent that is active on real estate transactions, but not the type the investors are interested in. For example, an agent may be a single-family home specialist but know little about duplexes, triplexes, or distressed properties. You will waste your time if that happens to you. Successful agents stay in their lane. They usually specialize in one or two property types, and most do not specialize in investment properties. So, it is up to you to narrow down the field.

The first step is to find the agent that specializes in the investments that interest you. Go to the MLS if you have access or Zillow if you do not, and search for brokers who have consistently listed pre-foreclosures, short sales, and REO (bank-owned properties). Traditional real estate agents run away from distressed properties. If you see an agent that lists short sales, REO, and foreclosures, they are investor-friendly. If you know an agent is listing a "fixer-upper," "TLC," or "cash sale only," the chances are that agent is investor savvy enough to know the game of investing.

The second thing you should look for when you are going through the list of the last fifty transactions is real estate agents consistently listing renovated properties. If you see that every house the agent lists is renovated, almost brand-new, the reason is that they are working with investors.

REAL ESTATE INVESTOR ASSOCIATIONS

You should also attend a Real Estate Investor Association (REIA) meeting in your area. The meeting will have all types of real estate investors, with investor-friendly agents. Nine times out of ten, they are there because they want to network with investors.

FACEBOOK

The final place to find an investor-friendly real estate broker is on Facebook. Join every investor group in your area that you can think of on Facebook. Then you can post something like, "Hey, are there any real estate brokers in the group interested in working with investors?"

You want to promise the broker if they find you a distressed property that when the property is renovated, you will list it with their firm.

WHAT EXPERIENCE SHOULD YOUR AGENT HAVE?

Most new investors feel that they want the most experienced agent. They want an agent that has been around for ten to fifteen years or so—someone that knows the business and can go to work for you. That makes sense on the surface. But there is an issue with that way of thinking as those agents are usually not suitable for investors. Many seasoned, experienced real estate agents do not often dedicate time to finding investor deals. To get great deals, you must act quickly (paddle faster). When you see a house pop up on MLS, you must set up a showing, drive to it, view the house, write an offer, and sign it through DocuSign, all within hours. A seasoned agent is working on many deals and often does not have time for an immediate response. If you must wait two days to see a house because your agent is busy and then wait another day to write a contract because they are busy, then this is not the agent for you. You have just lost the deal. You will not execute an agreement if you must wait two to three days, sometimes even a day, for your agent to respond to you. The busy agents, these experienced agents—it is not their fault. They are not doing anything wrong. They just do not have time to show the property right away, let alone write a contract on your behalf. They do not have the time to do things as quickly as an investor needs them done to make sure they have secured the deal.

The answer is not to be afraid to engage with newer agents. Of course, you want an agent who knows what they are doing, one that can write a contract, set up showings, one who has some experience. But they do not have to have five- or ten years' experience. You want an agent that has "time"—time to look for deals for you and time to scour MLS so they can set up showings right away. They can meet you at the property in a half-hour or hour. In other words, you want an agent that is hungry and wants to get the deals done. Maybe you are one of only four or five clients they are working with. They can work for you and spend much time trying to get offers submitted, showing properties to you quickly, and looking for deals for you if they are not working with many clients.

The other thing that is especially important is that the agent should be tech-savvy. Some seasoned agents have trouble with technology, with keeping up with computers and real estate databases. Some are great at it and some are not. Newer, younger agents might be excellent in this area, having been brought up in it. Older agents may suffer from a lack of knowledge on the subject. But with MLS systems, most can be set up so the agent can search it for you and automatically email you the listing the moment it hits the MLS. For example, if you have a wish for all listings of houses under $175,000 with three bedrooms, one bath in ZIP code such-and-such, it can be set up so they are automatically sent to you. Some agents do not know how to set those up, and some agents are too lazy to learn. So, if you have a tech-savvy agent that can do this for you, it is a massive benefit to you.

If you are hunting properties using Zillow.com or Realtor.com, those sites can be delayed for days before new listings appear, when a house is returning to the market, or when a house is going under contract. You cannot rely on those sites alone to find you great deals. So, you want an agent that has time, a tech-savvy agent, and an agent who is hungry and willing to work for you to find those deals.

The other thing that happens a lot to investors is that they can burn out their agents. If an investor is making fifty offers a month at fifty percent below asking price and is never getting offers accepted, then it will be difficult to keep your agent. They are going to think of you as a time waster and there will never be any deals consummated at offers that low, and you are spending hours of their time with no results. It is not wrong to make low offers, but you must be selective on how the offers are made. Look for aged listings for those low offers. Usually, a fifty-percent offer will rarely be accepted.

There you have it, the two significant steps you will need to take to make your first investment in ninety days or less. The first is your listing sources, while the second is the all-important investment-savvy real estate broker. To help you skim through the listings and quickly decide what is not a good deal, you can use the cost per square foot when you compare one property to another.

How to Know a Good Deal

You can always recognize a good deal if you understand the property's price per square foot. There are a great many bargains and good deals for sale in the market. They are easy to spot if you use the price-per-square-foot measure. This method will help you quickly find the best deals and the best bargains to take care of you and find your winners in the real estate game. To use it, you are only going to need to do one mathematical calculation: find the property's price per square foot. With this simple-to-use formula, you will flag all the good deals.

The first step is to know the average value per square foot of the local area you are surveying. You can Google the area (county or town) you are interested in and ask what the price per square foot is. It is essential as there are only two numbers to focus on—the price of the property and its square footage. To do this, you will need a calculator. Simply enter the sales price of the property, then divide it by its square footage. The answer is the price per square foot. If the price per square foot is fifteen to twenty percent lower than the average for the area, that property needs further analysis as it may be the deal you are looking for.

To find good deals, you need to become familiar with the price per square foot in your area. It is that simple.

SUMMARY

As you have found, there is no lack of sources of potential real estate leads that you can use to find your first investment. As you look them over, you will want to narrow them down to just three or four. However, if you discover an investment-oriented real estate agent as recommended, you may not even need that many. The agent should be sending you potential deals automatically by email while helping you screen those that do not fit the criteria you have set up with him.

All investors know that finding the right properties is the most time-consuming part of investing. It is constant research, property visits, telephone calls, and meetings. Those that are successful have the tenacity and patience to see it through. The website connectedinvestors.com reports there are 2.2 million real estate investors in this country using its best estimate to give you a boost.[3] They break down the number of people who own multiple investment properties as follows:

- More than one property: 10,200,000
- More than three properties: 1,042,157
- More than four properties: 547,947

It should show to you that although finding the right investment may be difficult, millions have done it and are doing it now just as you read these words. So, it is time to join them, too; get going and paddle fast.

NEXT STEPS

Now that you have learned how to find potential investment properties, you need to know how to analyze them to discover their cash flow and likely cash on cash returns. More importantly, you need to know what you should pay for them to make sure you are not overpaying. In the next chapter, we go over the financial rules of thumb and the methods you will use to examine the rent roll and financial numbers of a property. When you complete that chapter, you should be able to compete with most experience investors in finding and analyzing property investments.

CHAPTER SIX

STAY FINANCIALLY FOCUSED USING SIMPLE, YET USEFUL RULES OF THUMB

"Real estate investing can make you wealthy, and it can make you wealthy faster than any other investment out there, if you are willing to work toward it. And that's the key: work."
—Brandon Turner

A few years ago, the Founders Club of a small town in Mississippi held its annual event promoting education. For the event, it was decided to make it a mathematics contest with the winner awarded a $5,000.00 scholarship. Twenty-two high school students signed up for the contest that year. One of the students who was minding his eleven-year-old brother Billie took him along to the Founders Hall where the competition was held.

The Proctor passed out pencils and paper to everyone, including Billie, not realizing he was not one of the contest's participants. It seemed the contest challenge was not too difficult, but rather lengthy to perform. The Proctor asked the group to put their names on the top of the paper, then directed them to begin by using a sequence of numbers of one through one hundred, adding the lowest and highest numbers together, then the next lowest and highest, and total the result. For example, add 1 and 100, 2 and 99, and so on.

The group eagerly began, writing down numbers and adding, writing, and adding. But a few minutes into the exercise, Billie got up from his seat, walked to the front of the room, and handed in his paper. Not even five minutes had occurred. As the rest of the test-takers struggled on, Billie returned to his seat to wait for his brother to finish.

The next morning, Billie's parents received a call from the club's director asking if they could bring Billie to their next business meeting. When Billie and his parents arrived, the three-member contest committee questioned Billie on his answer. The director stated that there was some suspicion among the members about how Billie got his answer so quickly and asked him to explain it.

Billie eagerly spoke up. "It wasn't hard," he explained. "I noticed that when, as I added a few pairs of numbers together, they all equaled one hundred and one, so I just multiplied one-oh-one by the fifty combinations, and the answer came out five thousand and fifty."

"That's amazing," the chairman replied as the other two committee members scratched their heads in unison at his novel approach. That year, Billie's shortcut earned him the Founder's Club education prize—he was the youngest in its history to receive it—along with the consternation and begrudging admiration of all of those involved.

A note on this chapter. It is explaining the financial property analysis shortcuts and rules of thumb you must know. It is one of the most important. It is also the one I decided to skim through when I was reading my first book on investing in real estate. A combination of letter abbreviations and math caused my brain to immediately say, "Eh, I'll figure it out as I go." I then spent a great deal of time looking at potential properties unnecessarily wondering, "Is this one a good deal?" The material to follow is essential. Once you learn it, it can significantly lessen your property research time, ensure you are successful in your investments and keep you out of the zone of buyer's remorse. At first glance, it can seem dry, but as Billie showed the Founders Club, we provide you with analytical shortcuts that are not difficult to learn and apply. Following these guidelines will set you above the average amateur to ensure you are investing like a pro. It will also help when speaking with other investors; rather than nodding in agreement to a bunch of nonsense you do not understand, you will be able to move forward in conversations and potential deals.

If you want to hit home runs on your multi-family investments consistently, then you must learn about their basic financial structure. The understanding of its economic structure is the only way you can make an offer that will ultimately prove profitable in the long run.

The key to paying the right price for an investment property is through proper financial analysis. You do not want to overpay. For the price you pay will discover whether you will get the best return on your investment. This chapter will show you just how to perform real estate value analysis and find different real estate comparisons to decide the reasonable price of the income property. Using these techniques, you will ensure you are not overpaying, and this approach to real estate market analysis will help identify rental properties listed below market value.

In real estate jargon, the first thing you will ask from the seller or seller's broker is the property's "setup." Sounds cool, right? This term is shorthand for its financial documents. It includes two critical pieces of information: its rent roll and net operating income (NOI). From these pieces of information, we are then going to decide something called the capitalization rate, the debt coverage ratio, and finally, the purchase price.

The rent roll is the property's rental price and terms history. It does not have to be in any fancy format. It is just a written history of what the property has rented. It should also reveal how long the tenants were there. I will provide some more information on that later with examples.

Not all owners will have this information, especially if it is a single-family home. So, you will have to calculate this data yourself from the information supplied by the seller. There are examples of what you will need in the pages to follow.

THE NOI, OR NET OPERATING INCOME

The NOI, or net operating income, is simply a standard formula to find out the actual expenses and income for a specific piece of property. Because I like to be quick and lessen mistakes, I keep a sheet of fill-in-the-blanks that I can plug-in the numbers on for any property.[1]

Those two sheets of information are what you need for the base of a substantial investment. I am going to explain the specifics below. Still, if you understand that looking at current rent rates, rental history (rent roll), and how much the place will make for you (NOI), you can calculate to ensure you're making an offer you will be happy with on purchase.

The beauty of following these numbers is the peace of mind during your first few deals you may not get if you're focusing on market value, location, inflation, and all the other things people mention when they talk about real estate. When I was searching for my first deal, my dry erase board looked like I was trying to solve the da Vinci code. "Will yellow houses be more desirable in this area? Will it matter the neighbor does not cut his grass often? Oh, this one has a park nearby, that is nice unless the park users are too loud, and the like." You can temporarily shut down that part of your brain for your early assessments when you stick to the numbers.

Should you ever stretch the numbers? What if you believe you can eventually make the property profitable with rent increases, because there is a new hospital being built just down the street or (insert reason here)? Then sure, you can stretch your offer and reach toward the seller's asking price. But do not fall into the trap of falling in love with the property. Instead, learn to fall in love with the numbers.

That is why it is best to do this analysis before you tour the property. Ask the seller or broker to email or fax the setup information before you venture out. It will save a lot of wasted time. By examining the numbers first, you will know if you want to take the tour. I learned to take joy in just shutting down properties immediately on reviewing the documents. It made me feel the power I imagine a DMV worker feels every day.

The technique taught here will allow you to discover the right price to pay quickly. You must make offers rapidly because most investment properties are priced higher than a seasoned investor would pay. There are many more rejected proposals than accepted ones. Therefore, you want to send out as many offers as you can. It makes a 15-minute offer calculation a valuable tool in your purchase arsenal.

Let us go over what you are looking for in the rent roll and your NOI. If you have already forgotten what those are, it is all right, and we are about to go over them in greater detail.

THE RENT ROLL

There is a warning. Not all properties will have complete data or any data at all. That being the case, you must rely on your local research or broker estimates. Once you receive or calculate the documents, you will scan the rent roll. In examining the rent roll, you must decide if the numbers reflect market rents. How? I like to use online sites such as rentometer.com and Zillow.com that show rental histories for other houses in the area. Craigslist is also helpful. I will often test the market with a dummy Craigslist ad to check the response to a rent rate. Other alternatives include asking local property managers or looking at rental classifieds.[2]

What if the rents are under market? Great! After your purchase, you can bring them up. That will improve your cash flow and the value of your new investment. In older properties, you will find that rents are under the market. That is because owners often fear "vacancies" because of rent increases. Vacancies mean work and unwanted expense. A tip, though, unless your market is particularly saturated with rental properties, raising the rental price to within the current margins will not increase your vacancies.

You may ask yourself, "How do I know these numbers are not intentionally inflated to sell the property?" It is a good question. In theory, the people selling investment properties are investors and know what numbers buyers are looking for. The answer is that you are going to do your due diligence later, by examining the leases. For now, however, it is fine to base your first calculations off the rent roll they provide you or that you have estimated in your market research.

Below is an example of a rent roll of a two-family investment property I own.

76 High Street
Rent Roll
As of April 1, 2016

Apt. No	Name	Security	Rent/Mo.	Tenant Pays	Moved In	Lease Term
1st Fl.	Grace Mack and Jon William	$2,925.00	$1,950.00	Utilities. Plus 50% water bill plus snow removal	5/1/14	5/1/16 – 4/30/17
2nd Fl.	Mary Aronia	$2,475.00	$1,650.00	Utilities + 50% water bill	4/1/15	4/1/16 – 3/31/17
	TOTAL	$5,400.00	$3,600.00[1]			

(1) Monthly rent of $3,600 x 12 months = $43,200 annual rent

Table 6. Rent roll for 76 High Street, a two-family residential property.

Let us break down what we are looking at.

Tenant rent. You want to examine the tenant rents. Are they at market rent, or are they below the market? If the rents are low, can you raise them to improve the cash flow? Discover how long tenants have kept the same rent level as well as how often the rents were raised.

Tenant longevity. The rent roll often lists the tenant move-in date. If not, ask the seller for the information. The longer a tenant has stayed in an apartment, the more stable the property, and thus the less risk. If you find that tenants only stay for a year or less, that can be a cause for questioning the investment. You need to discover why the occupancy is short. It could mean maintenance issues, tenant conflicts, neighborhood problems, or similar reasons. A short occupancy is a red flag needing a bit more analysis, but not right now. Now is number-crunching time to come up with an offer within 15 minutes. It means we must find out what capitalization rate or cap rate (do not worry, I will go over what it is soon) to use based on the investment risk. We use the cap rate to discover the property value.

Tenant security deposits. Examine the tenant security deposits. In Table 6, they total $5,400. Why do we care about security deposits if we are going to have to return them to the tenants eventually? You care because you can use them to your advantage since the security deposits are turned over to you at closing. Almost every state has laws about protecting a tenant's security. Some even require that they are kept in an interest-bearing account for the tenant. Keep in mind, you will need to make that amount up in the future after you close. But the technique works to reduce your immediate cash outlay.

Here is an example. Assume the purchase price is $340,000, and you have obtained an 85-percent bank mortgage of $289,000. That means you are paying the seller $51,000 cash at closing besides the funds from your new mortgage. But, by netting out the $5,400 security deposits you will receive, your cash to the seller is just $45,600.

NET OPERATING INCOME (NOI)

Back to net operating income, usually stated as NOI. Net operating income is the measure of profit from an investment property calculated from its income statement. It is the total operating revenue minus the total operating expenses. (This is where I stopped paying attention the first time I was learning these subjects.) It is the income or earnings before interest and taxes are deducted. It does not include mortgage payments.[3]

All right let us go over what that means and how to calculate it. Table 7 shows a two-family income statement (setup) from one of my New Jersey duplexes. The amounts reflected are annual.

You may notice the line, "less vacancy of 6 percent." It is the number we will subtract to account for the time you will not have rent coming in, such as turnover between tenants.

Laundry income is what you can make by having coin-operated machines that require payment to use. Note how much it is in this case—$3,200. Little things like that can make a big difference in your final calculation.

Maintenance is either the amount provided by the previous owners that they have spent on maintenance and repairs or a number you come up with by reasonably estimating what the cost of maintenance over a year is going to be. Looking at things like the age of appliances and the interior condition can help you calculate this number. However, in this case, I used a "rule of thumb" of 10 percent of operating revenue. You should use that if you are uncertain of the owner's figures.

A management fee is what you would pay a management company to take care of the property instead of you. For a small property, 8 to 10 percent is a good rule of thumb. Always include this expense even if you plan to manage the property yourself. That is because your lender will insist that this expense be included when you apply for financing.

Professional services include things such as lawn care and technicians to set up phone lines and Wi-Fi. Again, these can either be provided by the previous owner or estimated by you.

76 High Street
Income Statement
As of April 1, 2016

INCOME:

Rent income	$43,200
Less vacancy (6%)	(2,592)
Laundry income (add this)	3,200
Operating revenue	$43,808

EXPENSES: (you're subtracting these things)

Property taxes	$12,300
Insurance	$1890
Maintenance (10%)	$4381
Utilities (tenants pay these)	
Trash removal (included in taxes)	
Management fee (8%)	$3504
Professional services	$945
Total operating expenses	$23,020

NET OPERATING INCOME (your projected income minus expenses = NOI) $20,788

ADJUSTED NOI say $21,000

Table 7. The income statement (setup) for a two-family residential property.

GETTING DOWN TO BUSINESS

So now you have this sheet of numbers, and you need to do some necessary calculations. The first is finding out the capitalization rate (cap rate). The second is the net operating income (NOI). Next, you want to determine the property's cash flow, and you will want to know its debt coverage ratio. This is what your lender will calculate to find out, in part, whether you qualify for a mortgage. Therefore, you need to know this before talking to a lender. The NOI is a number that will be used by your mortgage lender, too. We are going to break each of these down below using the same example from Table 7.

THE CAP RATE

The Cap rate is short for the capitalization rate. It is a standard measurement of real estate value used to compare real estate investments. The cap rate is the ratio between the net operating income of an income property and the purchase cost of ownership or its current market value.[4]

The cap rate will be the expected return on your investment capital if you pay all cash for a property.

Even more basic, here is another way to look at it. How much money would you need in the bank to earn $10,000 a year in an account where earned interest is 5 percent?

By dividing $10,000 by 5 percent, the answer result is $200,000. So, if the bank offers a 5 percent annual interest return, then you would need a deposit of $200,000 to earn $10,000 of interest yearly.

That 5 percent interest rate in real estate values is known as the cap rate. In real estate, the cap rate is not a fixed formula; it varies depending on the property's risk factors. What risk factors are you looking at? Maybe a great deal of tenant turnover, or a property that is expected to need a lot of repairs. These are 'risks' because they are going to decrease your potential income from the property. However, a property that is going to need repairs will also cost less and, therefore, yield higher returns. When you (or the mortgage lender) are calculating a cap rate for a rental property, it is going to be a lower rate for high-quality properties (often 2 to 4 percent), and a higher cap rate for lower-quality or smaller properties (usually 8 to 10 percent). The range of rates is based on the investment risk.

The higher the quality of the property, the lower the risk. It is that simple. Why does all this matter? Once you calculate your desired cap rate, you can calculate your maximum purchase price, and you are ready to make a reasonable and well-judged offer.

CALCULATING PURCHASE PRICE

We have the numbers we need; we can calculate the purchase price (highest offer price) with the easy-to-use formula below.

$$\text{Purchase Price} = \frac{\text{NOI}}{\text{CAP Rate}}$$

$$\text{Purchase Price} = \frac{\$21{,}000 \text{ (Table 7)}}{\text{Say } 7\%}$$

Purchase Price = $300,000

CASH FLOW

Do you remember when we calculated the NOI and left out our mortgage payments from the calculation? Well, cash flow will account for the mortgage payments.

$$\text{Cash Flow} = \text{NOI} - \text{Mortgage Payment}$$

Let us calculate the cash flow. Assume we can get a mortgage of 80 percent of the purchase price.

Purchase Price $300,000 x 80% = $240,000 Mortgage
Assume mortgage terms of 30 years fixed and 4.5% interest.
That calculates to be $1,216.00 a month or $14,592 per year.

(Note: this calculation was made using an online mortgage amortization site: https://www.amortization-calc.com/mortgage-calculator/)

Therefore, cash flow = $21,000 − $14,592 or $6,408

CASH-ON-CASH RETURN

You will want to know what return you would receive on your money if you bought this property.

Cash Down Payment	$60,000
Closing Costs (3%)	$1,800 (Estimated)
Total Cash Invested	$61,800

$$\textbf{RETURN} = \frac{\text{Cash Invested}}{\text{Cash Flow}}$$

$$\textbf{RETURN} = \frac{\$61,800}{\$6,408}$$

$$\textbf{RETURN} = \textbf{10.3\%}$$

Based on our calculations, if you purchase the property at $300,000, your cash on cash return slightly exceeds 10 percent. Just as a rule of thumb, you want to avoid investing in a property below a 10 percent return, and my target is 15 percent, as yours should be. However, at 10 percent, the numbers still look good, so I would be ready with the $300,000 offer.

However, we should also calculate the debt coverage to make sure our lender will agree with us.

THE DEBT COVERAGE RATIO (DCR)

In real estate investing, the debt coverage ratio is a measure of a property's financial capacity to cover its debt and meet its financial obligations, such as interest payments. A high debt coverage ratio will make it easier to make interest payments on the mortgage. This factor is what your bank will be the most interested in when deciding to approve your mortgage application.[5]

The debt cover ratio, also known as debt service coverage, is the ratio of NOI to the annual mortgage payment. The debt coverage ratio (DCR) or the debt service coverage ratio (DSCR) is the ratio of the NOI to the annual debt service you need to pay.

$$DCR = \frac{NOI}{Annual\ Debt\ Service}$$

$$DCR = \frac{\$21,000}{\$14,592}$$

DCR= **1.44**

The mortgage lender usually looks for a DCR of at least 1.25. But experienced investors shy away from deals that have a 1.25 to 1.40 DCR. That is because a DCR of 1.25 shows the property is producing only 1.25 times the debt coverage. Look for a property with a DCR of 1.4 or more. See the example above with a DCR of an excellent 1.44.

To stress, if you were producing a $100,000 NOI and you owed $80,000 in annual mortgage payments to the bank, you would pay the $80,000 mortgage 1.25 times over. To reiterate, make sure you make a safe investment on a one-to-three-family property by having a DCR of 1.40 or above.

DEBT TO INCOME REQUIREMENTS (DTI)

The DTI is not about the property you are analyzing, but it is about your finances. The ratio the lender's loan underwriter will use as part of the analysis of whether it will qualify you for a loan. The DTI is the ratio of what you owe to what you earn. The aim is to have a low DTI. The lower your DTI, the better it will help you qualify for the lender's lowest interest rate. Your ceiling should be 36 percent. You want to stay below that ratio. If you move past that number, you will be a risky borrower. That means higher interest rates for you. If your DTI reaches 45 percent, you will not qualify for a mortgage.

THE ONE PERCENT RULE

This rule is not to be used as your only method of property analysis. But it is a quick way to decide if a property will produce cash flow (a rule of thumb). For example, if the property's purchase price is $200,000, the property would need to pay a monthly rent of $2,000 to meet the 1-percent requirement ($2,000 divided by $200,000), which reveals a rough estimate of the property's break-even. If it is less than one percent, it will not provide a positive cash flow. You will want to walk, perhaps even quickly trot, away. If it is more than 1-percent, that will be a good indication of positive cash flow. You should then perform a full analysis based on the techniques shown in this chapter. But you can use the one percent rule method as your baseline metric to quickly decide if a deal looks good or not.

USING REAL ESTATE COMPARISONS (COMPS)

Finding the right purchase price can make or break an excellent real estate investment. It encompasses proper financial analysis along with market analysis, your intuition, and proper planning. The best way to calculate your offer price, low enough for a return, yet high enough for a competitive offer to win buyer acceptance is through analyzing real estate comps. It requires research and experience.

Comps are shorthand for property comparisons, properties in the same neighborhood that can be compared by age, condition, size, and features to the property you are trying to compare to. Learning how to use comps is invaluable for discovering the competitive asking price.

This method uses five parameters to find out a property's market value. These are the size in square feet of the property, the number of bedrooms and baths, its amenities, the neighborhood, and recent sales prices.

> **Home square footage.** It would be impossible to find properties with the exact square footage of the property

you are comparing to. So, you want to use properties that are at least 25 percent of the property you are analyzing. For example, if your property is 2000 square feet, you would look for comps in the 1,500 to 2,500 square foot range. Using a wider or smaller range will skew your averages.

Bedrooms and bathrooms. The number of bedrooms and bathrooms is especially important when combined with the square footage. For example, there could be a 1,500 square foot house with two bedrooms and one bath, while there could be another house of similar size but with three bedrooms and two bathrooms. The two different-sized properties would have different values if they were in the same neighborhood.

You can see that it is vital that you are comparing properties with the same number of bedrooms and bathrooms. If there are not any recently sold homes in the neighborhood with a comparable number of bedrooms or baths as the property in question, consider the property's amenities to make up for it.

Amenities. Amenities are features of the property that add or detract property value. For example, a pool, finished basement or attic, or screened porch. Finding properties with similar amenities is especially essential if you had difficulties identifying homes with the same number of bedrooms and bathrooms.

Neighborhood. The old saying "location, location, location" is never more critical than when you are making an investment purchase. You are not only investing in a property but a neighborhood. There are large swings in value from one block to another. The more amenities around you, the higher the rent. Renters want good amenities such as better schools, transportation, shopping, and restaurants.

An example is an apartment in a downtown area that will rent for more than a sleepy neighborhood many blocks away. A property's location impacts not only the home's value but also your ROI. While reviewing a location, discover the answers to the following:

- Who are the neighbors? Is the neighborhood made up of primarily of homeowners, first-time, retirees, or college students?
- What is it like at night? Is it a safe area?
- What about the noise level?
- Is the grass cut in yards on the block?
- Are most of the residents, homeowners, or renters?
- Are the homes in the area well-maintained?

Recent sale prices. The next step in comp comparisons after finding a half-dozen or more properties with similar square footage, bedrooms, bathrooms, and amenities are to find out how they are priced and how long they have stayed on the market. It will give you an idea of the price bracket you need to remain within to be competitive with the other properties on the market and increase your ROI.

> When reviewing prices of home sales prices, you must also consider the condition of the home, how near it is to schools and shopping, and area economics such as area growth, interest rate, property upgrades, and expansion potential.

USING COMPS TO DETERMINE VALUES

Now is the time to search for comparable properties of recently sold listings in your area. These are properties that have sold in the last six months. Make sure the comps you are looking at:

- Are in the same neighborhood
- Have similar features
- Are about the same square footage
- Are similarly built

Confirm your research with a reputable real estate agent in the area and corroborate the comps with him. The goal is to find three properties that are alike to help you in making your competitive offer.

RENTS AND VACANCIES

There is an excellent site to help you find out market rent for the neighborhood you are interested in at rentometer.com. This site provides a detailed rent comparison analysis in seconds. With it, you can analyze recent rental listings in the neighborhood. It calculates rent prices based on the property's location and apartment size and provides a market rental rate estimate. To use the site, put in the place where your property is found. Plug the number of bedrooms and bathrooms into the form. The results will estimate how much the rent is for each of them. The tool provides a rent range, the lowest, and the median.

The number of vacancies and the time a rental remains empty is critical in your analysis. A vacancy negatively affects rental prices. As an example, when there is a long time between renters, the rental rate usually decreases to attract more people to rent the property as soon as possible.

Vacancies can be one of the most significant expenses an owner can have as empty units do not pay. So, you must find out the type of vacancy you can expect in your property analysis. But finding these figures is not so easy. Unlike rentometer.com, there is no website that you can check with to see this specifically. However, there are ways around this. Here are three of them:

> **The Census.** The Census Bureau tracks and publishes quarterly vacancy rates for all 50 states and the 75 largest housing markets in the U.S. This information can be found on their website: https://www.census.gov/housing/hvs/data/rates.html. Although this is solid, evidence-based data, unfortunately, it cannot give you a detailed snapshot of a specific neighborhood or area you are researching.

> **Ask your agent.** You can ask them for a market analysis of rental statistics for your chosen area. They can use the MLS to show how long a property was vacant, and how the original list price compares with the price of the

property once it is rented. Of course, the limit here is that this will only provide you with info on properties that are currently listed on MLS.

Interview a property manager. The most accurate way to get the vacancy information is by questioning area property managers. They live and breathe vacancies. They can even tell what areas have the highest occupancy rates.

	Metropolitan Statistical Area	First Quarter 2020	Margin of Error[1]
	Akron, OH..	10.2	9.2
	Albany-Schenectady-Troy, NY.................	7.9	6.7
	Albuquerque, NM...............................	4.3	2.8
	Allentown-Bethlehem-Easton, PA-NJ..........	4.5	5.9
**	Atlanta-Sandy Springs-Roswell, GA[1]........	6.9	2.5
	Austin-Round Rock, TX........................	6.4	4.1
*	Baltimore-Columbia-Towson, MD[2]...........	4.7	3.3
	Baton Rouge, LA...............................	5.0	4.0
	Birmingham-Hoover, AL........................	20.6	7.4
*	Boston-Cambridge-Newton, MA-NH[3].........	6.8	2.3
	Bridgeport-Stamford-Norwalk, CT.............	5.1	5.5
*	Buffalo-Cheektowaga-Niagara Falls, NY[4].....	11.1	7.3
	Cape Coral-Fort Myers, FL.....................	9.4	10.4
	Charleston-North Charleston-Summerville, SC..	30.6	10.7
**	Charlotte-Concord-Gastonia, NC-SC[5]........	5.0	3.6
*	Chicago-Naperville-Elgin, IL-IN-WI[6].........	5.9	1.9
**	Cincinnati, OH-KY-IN[7].......................	5.4	3.8
*	Cleveland-Elyria, OH[8]........................	7.2	3.9
	Columbia, SC.................................	7.1	5.2

Table 8. A sample of the U.S. Census Rental Vacancy Rates for the 75 Largest Metropolitan Statistical Areas: 2015 to 2020.

CONCLUSION

Okay, we have discussed many formulas. We have looked at the rent roll. We learned how to calculate a property's net operating income (NOI). You saw how to find a capitalization rate (cap rate) based on the potential investment risk. After which you could find the purchase price to match that cap rate. Finally, you saw how to discover the debt coverage ratio (DCR) to ensure our investment return leaves plenty of room for interest. Some people are naturally numbers-oriented and take this information in with no problem at all. It is okay if you are not one of those people; it just needs a little practice. I can promise it becomes satisfying once you can briefly look at some facts and figures and decide whether you should give a potential investment any further thought or time.

To practice, you can go on any real estate website and find some multi-family properties for sale. Often, the seller will have listed much information to calculate the NOI. You can then make your best guess at filling in the other blanks and seeing what you come up with. When I first started practicing, I just so happened to find a neighborhood of properties that had high numbers. I assumed I was doing it wrong or that the information I read was just trying to trick me into thinking every buy was a great deal. However, as it turned out, that city was an excellent investment opportunity and is a great rental market currently.

These numbers are easy to calculate, and they tell you an incredible story. That is why I love multi-family investing. But hey, the formulas work just as well for single-family rentals, too. Please do not complicate or start to overthink your analysis. Rely on these formulas to guide you. You will realize how simple multifamily investing is with a little practice and by studying this chapter repeatedly. It will help you stay unemotional in your analysis.

Your primary objective is to decide an accurate purchase price. To do so, we rely on a precise calculation of net operating income (NOI). Unless it is a certified statement created by an outside accountant, it is often difficult to discover if the seller's NOI has been massaged. Questions on vacancies, missing expenses, or under-reported costs are not uncommon. So, it is best to add a reasonable expense contingency when you make your NOI calculations.

NEXT STEPS

Now that you know how to find out the values of properties that you might be willing to buy, you must convert them into winning offers to make those deals. The next chapter shows you what need to know to create successful offers, including some tricks of the trade that you can pull out when your offer may not be impressing your seller as much as you want it to.

CHAPTER SEVEN

HOW TO MAKE
WINNING OFFERS

"You must never try to make all the money that's in a deal. Let the other fellow make some money too, because if you have a reputation for always making all the money, you won't have many deals."

—J. Paul Getty

S ecretary of State James Baker was once asked at a Washington, D.C. diplomatic party to explain what shuttle diplomacy was.

Oh! It is unfailing, but a highly traditional negotiating method. Let me give you an example. Suppose you want to marry Rockefeller's daughter to a lad from a poor village.

Yes, Mr. Secretary, now how would you engineer such an impossible task?

Negotiation! I fly to whatever village, find a young man that lives there, and ask him, "Would you like to marry an American?"

He says, "Why?! We have such beautiful and comely young girls right here, and I have my choice!"

"Ah, yes I see, but did you know that this American is the daughter of a billionaire?"

He goes: "Oh, why didn't you say so! Well, this changes everything."

I then fly to Switzerland and meet with the board of directors of Switzerland's largest bank and ask, "How would you like to have a simple man be your bank's president?"

"Hölle nein! (translated: Hell no!)" they reply in unison.

"What if I told you he was Rockefeller's son-in-law?"

"Oh, why didn't you say so! Well, this changes everything."

So, then I fly back to New York and visit with Rockefeller and ask, "Would you like your daughter to marry a man from a village?"

"What do you mean? Everyone in my family is in banking."

"Funny you should mention that; he is the president of the largest bank in Switzerland."

"Oh, why didn't you say so! Well, this changes everything." "Abby, come here, my child. Secretary Baker found you a good husband. He is the president of Switzerland's largest bank."

"Bah! All big bankers are just weaklings or too feminine!"

And I say, "Well, this one is not."

"Oh, why didn't you say so! Well, this changes everything."

Making an offer when investing in rental real estate can be a remarkably simple process if, like Secretary James Baker, you know what to say and how to say it. But emotions, competition, and logic based on the wrong approach can make it complicated. The biggest question for the novice investor when starting is, "How do I make a real estate offer?"

When it comes to negotiation, some key elements come into play if you are going to be successful.

Life is all about negotiation. We do it subconsciously every day. The teen son negotiates when he wants to borrow the car. You negotiate as you discuss that unwanted invitation your wife wants you to accept. Even the dog negotiates with you for your time when he wants to go for a walk. We all do it. The question is, how best to do it when we are trying to buy an investment property?

The question is about how to get what you want. As a beginner, you are a bit hesitant about how to continue and what to say. That is understandable. But what is certain in life and negotiations is that if you do not ask, the answer is always no. You will get better deals by always asking. It is understanding how and when to ask that is the measure of a great negotiator.

This chapter will teach you how to make winning offers. It needs practice. But so, does everything worthwhile. Understanding negotiation concepts will give you the capacity to overcome seller objections and give you the ability to think on your feet to provide compromises leading to great deals.

FIND OUT WHAT THE SELLER WANTS

The key to negotiation is to understand what the other party wants. In investment negotiation, the other party will be the seller. The more information you can gain on the seller's needs, the better off you will be in settling on a price that will lead to a deal. If you do not know or your real estate salesperson does not, then ask the seller directly. Get the seller to tell you his story. That way, you can pick up on his needs so you can adequately address them.[1]

ASK FOR WHAT YOU WANT

Many years ago, when I was growing up as a skinny young high school kid in Westchester County, I was lamenting to an adult neighbor about my hesitancy to ask a popular girl I liked to the senior prom. I was so shy and wondered out loud about how I might make the first move. The neighbor looked me straight in the eye and sternly said, "Robert, if you don't ask, her answer is always no."

That advice was so shocking. It turned my thinking upside down and changed the way I approached the things I wanted. Every time I faced a challenge after that, I remembered, "If you don't ask, the answer is always no." It has served me well through life. I am happy to report that girl and I did go to the senior prom together that year. Because I learned how to build on the habit of asking, she is now my wife.

You might be surprised by how many times you will get what you want by simply asking for it. That is the first step in a successful negotiation. Asking prepares you for making the offer.

Another important lesson in learning what to offer is never to offer too much. Once your offer is made, you can never again offer anything lower. Your first offer must be based on real numbers, but also on what you calculate is right for a successful deal. The offer should be for what you want to get.

NEVER FEAR NEGOTIATION

The reason we fail to ask for what we want is our fear of rejection. Just as I was afraid to ask for the senior prom date, I feared to hear "no." Most sellers will not say no. Instead, they will counter your offer if they are interested in selling. The seller may not like the offer, or perhaps feel offended, but if the property is seriously for sale, there will be a price discussion rather than a confrontation.

You must not be fear asking for the price that will work for you, the amount that gives an adequate NOI, and cash flow. Support your offer using facts. If there is work to be done on the property, you can go through it with the seller. Let them know you are serious about the purchase and that your price is fair and based on the numbers. Real estate purchasing is all about back and forth until there is an agreement or until you must walk away.

THE OFFER TO PURCHASE

There are many ways a real estate offer may be formatted. It all depends on the deal you are trying to make and how complex it might be. The traditional offer will look something like the one that follows:

> **Names.** All contracts contain the names of the parties involved. In this case, it will be the buyers and sellers.
>
> **Dates and duration.** The agreement will be dated. The dates will include the start date of the contract as well as an expiration date. Dates of contingencies are listed, including the date of receiving financing from a lender.
>
> **Legal descriptions.** All real estate offers usually contain the meets and bounds property description. This is the legal description of the property that will eventually be placed on the deed. The legal description is made by a licensed surveyor whom the buyer employs and pays for. The surveyor is trained to decide the legal description in any area where the property is located.

Offering price and financial terms. This is the section in which your dollar offer is written with any special terms required to buy the property.

HOW TO FEND OFF MULTIPLE OFFERS

There will be times that you will be competing against other offers. It happens in a hot market. Many investors are waiting to jump on properties just like the ones you are interested in. If you are not prepared, you may find the ideal property that you thought was surely within your grasp has slipped out and is no longer yours. We have prepared several techniques that you can employ should this happen to you—and it will happen—so study them well, as they will come in handy.

OFFER MORE MONEY IF YOU CAN

Money is the easy answer to solving many a purchasing problem. If you know that there will be competition, include an escalation clause in your offer. This clause allows you to raise your price above a competitor's offer to a limit you set. However, if your budget is limited regarding the price, you might suggest increasing your deposit amount. It does not affect the sales price but does provide you with an excellent psychological advantage when your seller sees a traditional two-to-three-percent deposit jump to, say, ten percent. This act by itself will show how serious a buyer you are to the seller.

LOWBALL OFFERS

Market conditions will decide your ability to successfully present a lower offer—meaning if it is a buyer's or seller's market. With a buyer's market, it is common to put in an offer around ten percent below the asking price. In a seller's market, it is much more difficult to go below asking price, because inventory is low and multiple buyers are interested in the same properties.[2]

If a property has only been on the market for a day, it is not good to go in with a lowball offer. But if it has been on the market for a year with price decreases, then have at it. The longer a property has been on the market, the less of an upper hand the seller has in negotiation.

There is always a danger that a low offer will insult the buyer. The results leave such a poor impression with the seller there is never a counteroffer. The buyer often interprets such offers as disrespecting their property.

There are ways you can increase the likelihood that your lower offer might be accepted and increase the chances of negotiation.

If you want to try to pick up a property at a bargain price, a low offer could be just the way to achieve it. In this case, you might drop your offer to around twenty-five percent below the asking price.

Keep aware of current market conditions. For low offers to work, market conditions usually must be conducive. Check with your agent on local conditions to see if a low offer is a right strategy. A seller's market will likely cause your proposal to be rejected. The buyer has the advantage under those circumstances. But no matter the real estate market, a property that has been on the market for more than several months is likely to have its seller willing to negotiate a lower price.

If you take time out to study the real estate market before you make an offer, you can be far more successful by designing your offers to match market conditions. One seller might be happy to receive an offer, even a low one in a market, while another one will want to haggle back and forth on price. Lowball offers often result in sellers selling to someone else. So, you must be cautious with this offer, or you will wind up losing the property to someone with a higher offering price.

> **Be respectful of sellers.** No matter the market conditions and the circumstance, a lowball offer is bound to be upsetting to a seller. The seller had high expectations for the sale and now meets with an offer well below their asking price. How would you feel? After all, this is the home where the seller raised his family and made memories. It is bound to affect the mood of your seller. However, if you make your offer with expressions of your appreciation for the property, for example using a home offer letter, your offer is much more likely to be accepted than just a cold contract or negative comments about the property's condition. You get the idea.

Have your agent contact the listing agent. Another strategy that often works has the buyer stay out of the negotiation and use the help of their real estate agent to discuss the offer with the seller. Let your agent discuss your proposal with the listing agent before it is put into the seller. The listing agent can also tell you more about the sellers, such as their reason for selling and the other circumstances of the sale. This method depersonalizes the process and keeps you from the seller if they are upset about the low offer.

Have your financing in order. If you hope to have a low offer accepted, you must make sure your financing is in order. Make certain any offer you give is with a lender's preapproval letter and a cashier's check for the earnest money deposit. Remember, as we discussed earlier, the higher the deposit, the better. It is even more critical when you are making a low offer. Ten percent is an excellent target to shoot for. It confirms to the seller that this is a sincere offer that they should take seriously. By the way, lowball offers are most likely to be accepted if you are making all-cash offers with no financing.

Now take a time-out. Your finances should be in order at this stage. If you find you are stretching and you might be in trouble with property payment down-the-line, then be smart and walk away from the transaction. It is not worth the damage to your credit. Think about it, and if you offer to waive the property inspection to save money and pray that nothing of significance is found because you can't afford expensive repairs, this may not be the time to move forward on the deal. It is better to move on to a more affordable investment than to risk your ability to make a future investment.

Remove as many contingencies as possible. If you are making a low-price offer, you should not expect to load the seller with repairs and other expensive contingencies. You must still order a home inspection, so you are aware of anything significant or structural. You can use the report as your to-do list after closing.

Since the sellers agreed to a bargain sale price, keep the agreement simple, and avoid extra contingencies. At this great price, you should expect to close on the house in an "as-is" condition.

Be prepared to lose the house if your offer is too low. But if you can make a low offer respectfully, you could end with a great deal.

HOW A SELLER MIGHT JUDGE YOUR OFFER

When comparing offers, sellers usually consider the following:

- Purchase price
- Whether the offer is cash or needs financing
- If financing is needed, the loan type and the borrower's qualifications (i.e., whether they are preapproved)
- The closing date
- Conditions on the sale (for example, inspections or the sale of another property)
- Other costs that impact the seller's profit

STRONG OFFERS EQUATE TO SUCCESSFUL DEALS

Calculating the best offer to make on a property takes methodical work. Once you have determined the offer you will make, there are methods you can use to improve it in the eyes of the seller. These include such things as escrows, contingencies, and the size of the down payment, to name a few. Here are some suggestions to guide you through the process and help you decide your best offer.

HOW TO MAKE A STRONG OFFER

Here is what you can expect when you put in your first real estate investment offer. The process goes like this:

- Your real estate agent presents your offer to the seller
- Now the seller has three options:
    - o The seller accepts the offer.
    - o Seller declines the offer because the seller feels your offer was not close enough to expectations to negotiate.
    - o The seller presents a counteroffer, which might be a change in price and terms.
- You have three options if the seller counteroffers—accept, counter, or decline. You can carry on a back-and-forth negotiation until you have an agreement or walk away if a transaction fails.

When there is an acceptance, a contract for purchase is drafted, usually by the seller's attorney, and signed by both parties. This phase in the purchasing process is known as *under contract*. You now move to the contingency period. It is the time where all inspections, appraisals, and anything else contained in your purchase contract take place.

PICK A STARTING PRICE

It is just a number. It seems so simple, yet so much goes into the offer you begin with. You must consider your budget, market conditions, the seller's circumstances, the house maintenance, and other issues specific to the property. A local real estate agent can be your best friend in these circumstances. Not only will they take the mystery out of local conditions, but they can also offer a purchase strategy based on their experience. Now is the time to ask questions to zero in on your offer and listen to your agent's suggestions. After all, your agent wants you to make this deal as much as you do. He is there to offer his help.

GOING "ABOVE AND BEYOND"

Above and beyond is an excellent negotiating ploy. When you use it, you make the terms of your offer stand out. This can often seal the deal. As an example, you can offer to contribute $5000 toward the seller's closing cost. It will set your offer apart from the other offers a seller may be considering. Making the seller happy equates to winning the deal. Of course, such an offer depends on your available funds. You could also offer something more modest, but still, have it be impactful. You can add to your proposal, "that upon close of escrow buyers will contribute $500 toward the seller's moving cost."[3]

KEEP THE FINANCING CLEAN

Where financing is concerned, buying a property with cash is always attractive to sellers, if that is a luxury you can afford. Not many beginning investors can offer this seller leverage. Since a mortgage lender will not have to get involved, the sale becomes much easier, and there will be no worries that a loan will not get approved at the last minute. Cash is not an alternative for every buyer. If a mortgage is a must, make sure that you provide a preapproval letter, so the sellers know a lender has already vetted your finances.

OUTLINE THE CONTINGENCIES AND OTHER OFFER DETAILS

Contingencies are the clauses in your contract that give you an out if something unforeseen arises. They protect you from losing your earnest money and provide you with leverage to get the seller to help you deal with whatever comes up. Standard contingencies include mortgage financing, home inspections, and appraisal. They allow you to walk away or renegotiate if hidden issues are discovered.

Other contingencies that can be used to make a contract more attractive to a seller include a rapid closing. Also, it is not uncommon to rent the house to the seller while they locate a new home. The real estate agent will be helpful in suggesting contingencies that might add to the attractiveness of the contract of sale.

The "other costs" item includes a miscellaneous list of familiar costs. They might consist of asking the seller to pay for termite repairs, or repairs to items discovered in the home inspection, or a home warranty, or ask the sellers to credit you money towards your closing costs. Obviously, the more you need the seller to pay for the extraneous item, the less happy he will be. In a competitive market, you risk a seller's rejection when you ask for these items. You should absorb the cost and secure the deal.

BUY THE HOME "AS IS"

Selling a house "as is" means the seller will make no repairs or improvements and is selling the house in its current condition. As a buyer, it means you are buying the home in its present condition with no contingency for inspection. As the buyer, you will assume responsibility for all repairs.

It is a strong choice for a buyer to use to cement a deal. It is attractive from the seller's viewpoint because it lessens the seller's cost. So, if a seller is deciding between two offers made at the same price, he will find the "as-is" offer is financially more attractive.

If you wish to make this offer, you can still have an inspection. It will just be for informational purposes only as you will be responsible for repairs noted in the examination. You can always cancel the contract if major or more costly repairs are discovered.

THE ESCROW DECISION

A real estate escrow means putting something, such as a deed or money, in the care of a neutral third-party until certain conditions are met. Your contract will contain an escrow provision which describes, in part, who will hold the deposit money you offer. Your deposit shows to the seller that you are a serious buyer because, under the terms of traditional escrow terms, you lose your deposit if you do not go through with the contract. So, offering a more substantial than usual deposit to the seller will advance the value of your offer to the seller and may make the difference of you securing the deal in a competitive market.

Traditional deposits often range from one to three percent of the purchase price of the property. However, you will get your seller's favorable attention if you can offer five to ten percent. The escrow deposit is held by a third-party, usually the seller's attorney or in some states an escrow company.

SEND YOUR OFFER

Once you have gone through the financial details and your calculations, you are ready to have your real estate agent deliver your offer. After which you must patiently wait for the response. You have come a long way, and you should be proud of all you have succeeded until this point. Even if nothing comes of it this time, you gained courage and experience to go on to the next one. If you have suspenders, you can put both thumbs in them and stick out your chest as you have left the comfort of your nest and made it as a fledgling investor. All you need is the worm, your property.

Do you want to make your offer even more robust with a little effort? There is a growing tradition of offering personal letters with offers. It is known as the home offer letter. They are helpful in a competitive market where a property may receive multiple offers. A personal home offer letter sets your offer apart in the eyes of the seller. You can follow the sample letter we have prepared. Put it in your words for the best results.

Here are some helpful suggestions, with an example home offer letter to follow:

> Make your opener as personal as possible. Now it is time to check out that junk drawer to locate that long-forgotten ink pen. The ink pen (ban the ballpoint) is your secret weapon as it symbolizes "very personal." You will also want to use good stationery. If you do not have it around the house, make a trip to the store. After all, this is an important step. Get comfortable and take a moment to get yourself in a friendly and sincere mood as this will translate to your letter.
>
> Begin the letter. Now think about how you will begin the letter. If you do not know the owner's name, you can

still start on a personal note. You should avoid mentioning you are buying an investment. Try something like:

Dear owners of the charming, white Colonial Cape Cod with the lovely welcoming cherry tree in front,

Tell them about yourself. It is a difficult time for sellers. They are emotional, and many want their house, where they spent so many years, to go to someone who will appreciate it. Your letter should show them that. The letter drops the curtain on who the buyers are, the real people behind the offer. Your words should help them picture the buyer they were looking for whom wishes to care for their home.

Our names are Marvin and Grace. We have been looking in your neighborhood for several years trying to find that perfect house, and when we saw yours, we fell in love all over again. With its well-kept backyard, it is the ideal place for children, and the neighborhood schools could not be better. But best of all, Grace was raised in an almost identical house as yours, even down to the cherry tree out front that she used to climb as a little girl. It is the ideal place to raise a family.

Point out the property's qualities. Most sellers take pride in where they live, so if the house needs repairs, avoid those. Instead, write about the things that stand out and that you care about. It is time to add the compliments—we like to receive them. Take the time to point out a few things.

We loved your backyard patio and pergola, which make barbecuing outside a real attraction for us. Your hardwood floors are in such great shape for the age of the house, and we wondered how you keep them that way. We hope you will let us know your secret. We could tell that you have cared for that home. Marvin and I look forward to taking the same care of it, too.

Find a connection. Did you see anything familiar when inspecting the house that you might connect with? Were there photos or familiar knickknacks? Use those to make a connection in your letter.

We could not help noticing the photo in the hall of the graduation at Brown University. My mother grew up in Rhode Island and attended Brown, too. She studied design. We spent a lot of time at Narragansett Beach in the summers.

Explain your bid, especially if low. This is the spot where you convert the romance to an explanation of your numbers. It is important for low offers. You want to explain your offer at this stage rather than apologize for it. You do not need to go into cash flow analysis and cap rates. You want to stay away from that. Your letter might go something like this:

As we mentioned, we loved your home even though it was above our budget. It checks all our boxes, and the neighborhood is so attractive. We realize you are asking $X and respectfully ask if you would consider $Y. We would like to make this our dream house without adding crushing debt. We are both preapproved for our mortgage at that price and are flexible on a closing date. We hope we can work this out with you.

Close with many thanks. This is the portion of your letter to wind things up and put in your closing argument. Add flattery and show that you look forward to hearing back from them.

Thank you for your thoughtfulness in reviewing our offer. We look forward to your favorable consideration and the possibility of making your lovely home ours in the future. We thank you and hope to hear back from you soon.

If you followed the format, we provide there is a strong possibility that your carefully crafted letter worked. You now have an offer that has been accepted, and it is time for a high five. Off you go to your lender to convert your mortgage preapproval into a formal mortgage commitment.

SUMMARY

When it comes to negotiations and how to make those winning offers, some key elements come into play if you are going to be successful. The key to a successful negotiation is to understand what the seller wants. We discussed merely asking for what you want. If you do not ask, the answer is always no. We looked at the strategy for overcoming competition; sooner or later, you will be competing against other offers. One of the ways to successfully compete is to go above and beyond with your offer. When you use this technique, make the terms of your offer stand out in the eyes of the seller. This chapter also explained how to handle contingencies, as far as to when to include them and the best time to remove them from an offer. We went on in detail on how to make lowball offers, as well as the cautions you must take to prevent insulting the seller. We also went over buying as-is. It is a strong option for a buyer to use to cement a deal. It is extremely attractive from the seller's viewpoint because it reduces the seller's cost. Finally, we suggested the benefits of using the house offer letter to have your offer stand out and sway the seller in a competitive market. By following these suggestions, you will make more winning offers and better real estate investments.

NEXT STEPS

No book on real estate investment would be complete without discussing methods of negotiation. In the next chapter, we outline ways for you to take the winning advantage in negotiating with a seller to achieve what you want. So, read on and get ready to learn some exciting ways to improve your negotiating skills to buy your new investment.

CHAPTER EIGHT

NEGOTIATING; THE ART OF THE DEAL

In business as in life, you don't get what you deserve. You get what you negotiate.

—Chester L. Karrass

S ir Alexander Korda, the late British film producer, and director, while visiting Marc Chagall's studio, admired a painting that he said he would like to purchase. Chagall declared that negotiations about money embarrassed and upset him and promptly left the room, leaving Mme. Chagall to discuss the price. Leaning forward to speak with her, Korda suddenly noticed a reflection in the mirror. It was Chagall, standing, as he thought, unseen in the hall and signaling to his wife. He then sketched a dollar sign in the air, held up five fingers, then ten, and finally crossed his index fingers to indicate that she should multiply. Before Mme. Chagall could say anything, Korda offered $50,000. "Why that's the sum I was going to ask you for!" exclaimed Mme. Chagall in some surprise. "How did you guess?"

"Ah, madame, sometimes a painting simply speaks for itself."[1]

To prevail in a negotiation, you must know what the other party wants. In this whimsical story, Sir Korda was lucky enough to discover it early enough to make use of it. Our chapter on negotiation will explain the procedures one should follow to complete a successful real estate investment negotiation. But first, some background.

Mary P. Rowe, an Adjunct Professor of Negotiation and Management at the MIT Sloan School of Management, defines negotiation as "all interactions between two or more points of view. That is just about everybody all the time."

When Rowe began teaching negotiations in the spring of 1985, twenty years after the book *A Behavioral Theory* was published, she spent much of New Year's vacation rereading it and diagramming the various aspects of negotiation and how they interact. In the end, "I had two pages on different bargaining tactics and the various sources of power," she said. She began to build case studies and examples around her notes. "And, like hundreds of others, I found the platform simple and easy to understand once I had the bones and easy to apply in teaching and my professional work."[2]

3-D Negotiation Chart

Dimension	Focus	Obstacles	Approach
1st	Tactics (people & process)	• Interpersonal issues • Poor communication • Hardball attitudes	• Actions at the table • Improved processes and tactics
2nd	Deal design (value & substance)	• Lack of agreements	• Go back to the drawing board to design lasting deals
3rd	Setup (scope & sequence)	• Parties, issues do not support an agreement	• Make moves away from the table to create a more favorable environment

Table 9. The negotiation matrix designed by Mary P. Rowe.

The following negotiation strategies are time-tested real estate negotiation techniques to help you get the best real estate deals. The best negotiators are people that are very likable and nice to speak with. With that hint, be on your best behavior.

REAL ESTATE NEGOTIATION STRATEGIES

Reconnaissance. Studies have determined that when it comes to negotiation, the side with the best information has the best chance of prevailing. In real estate negotiations, knowledge equals power. You want to do every bit of research that you can to gain information about the other party and their property. You should research as many details as you can about the property. Go through public records. See if the property listing has expired or was a past expired listing. Check the size of the mortgage that is on the property. Low equity often means less negotiating room. You will want to know its days on the market. Look at the social media pages of the seller to see what you can learn from them. Sleuth out the motive for the sale of the property.

Call the listing agent and ask them questions such as:

- Should I expect other offers on the property?
- Is there much competition on the property?
- You may even ask what the motivation for the sale is.

Start crafting the offer. Negotiations begin when the offer is submitted. There are many strategies to do this. We describe what we think is the best way to make an offer in the paragraphs below. But the proposal should be crafted by the data that was found in the early inspection step. You need to remove emotion from decision making. You need to understand how much negotiating power you have at this stage. What is meant by negotiating power can be summed up in these examples. Say you found a charming home in a great location with a new kitchen and it is underpriced. The result is you will have a lot less negotiating power on that property than on a rural area property that has seen better days and has been on the market for over ten months.

In the example of the first property, to be successful, your offer must be crafted to be more conducive to the seller's terms. That might mean full asking price, avoiding asking for expenses, putting down a larger deposit. In the latter circumstances, you would make offers below asking price and ask for costs as well as repairs.

Submitting the offer. Submitting an offer during real estate negotiation is essential, and you need to realize how much bargaining power you have. Your goal should be to be the first person to put in an offer as it gives you a strong psychological advantage. Maybe you will be able to get your offer accepted first. Your offer should include a short expiration date (3 days or less) to push the buyer on a decision before your offer expires. If you get your offer accepted, the next phase is the second round of negotiation after your property inspection report has been concluded.

The second comes real estate negotiation. This phase is sometimes called the repair request; these are second-round negotiations. This phase involves renegotiating if you find things wrong with the property. It is best to negotiate the price down rather than have the seller agree to do the needed repairs. That is because there is little incentive to do quality work. On the contrary, the concern would be shoddy repairs now.

There is usually a time in negotiations for hardball tactics to get the price down even lower.

LEARN THE PSYCHOLOGY OF NEGOTIATION

Has it ever crossed your mind as to how you could improve your negotiation skills and become a better negotiator? If so, you will be pleased to learn that it is not as difficult as you may think. You can negotiate on the same level as the most accomplished negotiators if you learn the psychology of business negotiations.

Negotiation psychology sounds far more complicated than it is. But if you read on, you will find that it is made up of simple building blocks that are easy to understand once you understand the meaning behind the negotiation.

Mary Rowe of MIT, who was introduced earlier, explains, "When you think about the psychology behind negotiation, it means learning how to navigate diverse perspectives and expectations." She breaks down what seems to be a complicated subject into seven parts.

How To Negotiate a Deal

- Establish a solution for all those involved
- You must be prepared to walk away
- Be tactful with the words you use
- Only negotiate in person and not by phone
- Listening is more important than speaking. Listen carefully

- Concentrate solely on the result

There should be a seventh item added to this list, which Ms. Rowe neglected. Lockdown the offer with an escalation clause.

Even as a beginning investor, your early skills should see you through to positive results. As you gain experience, however, you will want to experiment with different strategies to improve your techniques so that you are making more deals on a more regular basis. Here are some practical, tactical lessons you can master over time.

THE WIN-WIN TACTIC

This top investment negotiating tactic benefits all parties. The method is known as the win-win tactic. As an example, you might offer to advance the seller's moving costs. In the grand scheme of things, this concession is a low cost to the buyer but would be of significant benefit to the seller. The seller would see that as both an unusual and generous concession, which could advance the negotiations to favor the buyer's offering price.

Experienced investors have a list of items to negotiate. They never pick just one. If you take the time to learn about the seller beforehand, as we suggested, then the list should be slanted to the seller's perspective. This homework will benefit you by determining the wants and needs of the seller and allow you to plan how to address them best. Being prepared will allow you to conduct negotiations where both parties get some of what they want.

THE ART OF THE COMPROMISE

Going with the win-win tactic is the method that compromise is made from. Perhaps you can suggest that you will clean up the junk in the backyard if the seller knocks a few thousand off his asking price. Or maybe, to push for a quicker closing date, you increase your offer. Just think through potential areas for compromise before you sit down at the negotiation table. Doing this work in advance avoids giving up too much or, worse, walking away from what could have been a good deal. Compromise makes for a useful bargaining chip, but so does holding your ground where it matters.

YOU MUST BE PREPARED TO WALK AWAY

There is a time in a negotiation that an experienced negotiator will have to push his chair back, get up from the negotiating table, and walk away. The walk-away is done when negotiations, in the opinion of the negotiator, come to an impasse. The seller must be convinced that you will walk away if the talks stagnate. The tactic is reinforced if the seller knows you have other investment properties you are looking at. So, the lesson here is to come to the negotiation with other properties in mind so if you must walk away, you can do so with confidence, knowing you can begin on a new deal. If the seller sees this confidence and understands he is not the only property you are working on, he will be more apt to accept your offer.

IF YOU NEED TO—ADD AN ESCALATION CLAUSE

The escalation clause should be added to your offer if you feel the seller will receive multiple offers on his property. The provision points out that you will pay some amount (though limited) above the highest of any additional offers the seller may receive. The clause caps this amount to make sure any increased amount does not exceed a specific price point. You should always discuss an escalation clause in a competitive market to assure that you will win the deal. You can read more about the escalation clause and see examples further on in this chapter.

ALWAYS USE POSITIVE LANGUAGE

Using affirmative language during negotiations is contagious. A positive approach gives you the mantle of a person who is direct and decisive. This style of approach is, in fact, a useful negotiating tool. You should avoid using negative words such as "not," and "I can't." You might state a negative in a positive sentence such as "The property needs its oil tank removed." That is a positive declaration for a negative subject.

Another example might be substituting "The property doesn't look maintained" with "The property needs renovations." It is stating the same action but in a much more positive way.

THE NEGOTIATION SHOULD BE CONDUCTED IN PERSON

It has become common to communicate by text and email in today's commercial world. It is perhaps the most common way of conducting business. However, negotiations are best performed in person when possible for many reasons, the first of which is that it is more polite and respectful of the other party. A sit-down helps to make sure that everyone is on the same page. Being face-to-face removes misinterpretations. Body language, which is often the best cue of how someone feels about a subject, can be read best at in-person meetings. For the best results in property negotiation, make sure you schedule an in-person meet and greet.

Of course, if the deal is long-distance or complicated schedules prevent it, an in-person negotiation may not be possible. But that is not an excuse to use email as it is too impersonal. Instead, use video conferencing. It is much better than the phone as, with a phone, you often have a static-filled phone line, and there is nothing more irritating than a voice-over-Internet line that echoes or has constant static or drops out. And with the phone, you cannot read body language.

THE KEY TO NEGOTIATION IS LISTENING

Judge Judy is renowned for telling her litigant, "You have one mouth and two ears; shut your mouth and put your listening ears on." It is a little harsh, but as TV's highest-paid daytime host, she must be doing something right. In negotiations, we can all follow her advice as listening is the key to a positive result. How destructive is it to have one person lose their temper and, in a huff, walk out? That is not the walkout we refer to above. It is a temper tantrum resulting from a misunderstanding. The misunderstanding is attributed to the lack of listening. It kills the deal and harms the reputation of the party that spouted off. Leave your ego outside and tuneup your ears for the best results during a negotiation.

ALWAYS CONCENTRATE ON THE PRIZE

Negotiation is all about the result. So always keep that goal in mind during the of your discussions. It is common to be distracted with counteroffers and unrelated issues when you should be focused on the purchase price. Refer to your talking points throughout the negotiation to make sure you have not missed anything. Keep your focus during the meeting and cite your notes when necessary to ensure you bring up each of your talking points. Make sure it is not you who is walking out of the negotiations only to remember that you forgot to resolve an important issue. It will not only be embarrassing, but it could be costly.

Do not let small points get in the way of your primary reason for being there in the first place. Those things can happen in a heated back-and-forth session. As an example, even though you had to give in on a closing date that you did not want to, you still hit the bullseye with the purchase price you wanted. Even though you did not get everything you wished for, you walk away with a great property.

NEGOTIATION PRESSURE POINTS

If the art of negotiating were just a simple system where you followed a few steps, then quick memorization would make everyone interested in it a negotiation expert. But it is not a science; it is an art. One of the terms of this art form is the negotiation pressure point. This phrase describes the various processes in a negotiation that influence its result. Just think about it as the different aspects of the deal that influence the outcome. It means that there are certain areas that you can concentrate on that affect the agreement. By learning these pressure points, you can change the outcome. So, though we mentioned that negotiation is not a system you can memorize, you can learn the pressure points to achieve negotiation success.

THE TIME PRESSURE POINT

When under the pressure of time, sellers become more flexible. You will receive a better deal if you have a motivated seller looking for a fast sale. Use the following examples to win the deal you want. Below are examples of time pressure points:

- Nearing foreclosure
- Underwater on their mortgage
- Relocating to a new job
- Closing on another property
- Going through a probate case
- Tax delinquent

This is just a small list of time pressure examples that can motivate sellers. As a good negotiator, it is up to you to do your homework to discover a seller's motivations before you begin negotiations and to discover the seller's pressure points.

Do not forget that negotiation, in part, is a traditional conversation between two parties—the buyer and the seller. It is a time to learn what you and the seller have in common and bond over that. Did you attend the same schools? Do you both love sailing?

You can find that you have something in common with the seller just by asking him. By asking questions, you are building a rapport. As an example, ask, how long have you owned the property? How many times has the tenant renewed his lease? Has the property been exterminated for termites? If so, when was the last time? Do the questioning slowly and meticulously, getting to know more about the seller. When you have shared that much time with a seller, they will feel more trustful of you and somewhat guilty. They will think that they must make a deal with this buyer, having spent so much time with them. When the seller feels like this, there will be no terms you cannot negotiate.

Time is your most powerful asset. Use it to your advantage.

IN REAL ESTATE NEGOTIATIONS, KNOWLEDGE IS KING

In negotiations, the person with the most knowledge comes out the winner. It should be you, as you have learned by now that you should be performing reconnaissance on your seller before you meet. The more you know, the better your chances of uncovering the seller's selling motives. However, there will be a time where you will need to ask direct questions of the seller. You might ask if there any back taxes owed or what the foundation crack is all about or the last time the roof was replaced. A seller's lack of response is still an answer, as there are undisclosed issues in the property.

Besides the seller, your investigation should continue with the neighbor, local investors, and of course, your broker. You will want to question anyone that can tell you about the property or its seller.

YOUR OPTIONS

The person with the most flexibility in a negotiation has the most power. This does not refer to the flexibility of terms in a deal but the flexibility to walk away. If you make it clear to a seller that you have other options besides his property, you are presenting the seller with a powerful pressure point. You must communicate that his property is just one of many you are considering. It gives you powerful leverage during negotiations.

Alas, be careful as this works in reverse, too. A seller can tweak you also by saying he has multiple offers on his property. The lesson here is not to focus too much on deal options, or the deal will not get done at all. You might tell the seller that you are considering other properties as a buyer, but only when suitable. Be confident in your negotiations. Learning the correct way to approach a negotiation pressure point will go a long way toward ensuring a successful career as an investor. Finally, alternatives are good not only for negotiating but also for your portfolio.

GENERAL REAL ESTATE NEGOTIATION TIPS

The last thing you want to say to your agent is that you are in a rush, as that could be used against you during negotiations. You also do not want to reveal how much you are willing to pay. Do not give them your top figure. Keep them guessing for the best results. An agent may take your top number and use it with other potential buyers, showing that they have a buyer willing to pay such and such to force a bidding war. You should not tell your agent that you just missed property purchase and that you are upset about it. Keep your emotions to you. Do not show any excitement. You must not allow the agent to know that you are willing to buy the property at any price. If they hear that from you, they will continually push you toward a higher price to try to get the highest amount. Do not tell the agent that you are unfamiliar with the market or have no idea what a property is worth. Do not disclose to your agent what your plans are for the property.

YOUR REAL ESTATE SECRETS

Giving your real estate agent too much information can cause you to pay a higher price for a property and put you in a situation where you lose some of your negotiating power. Here are the seven things not to reveal to your real estate agent so you will be in the best position when it comes time to negotiate.

If you want to negotiate the best deal, you need to understand how negotiating works. First and foremost, in the real estate world, buyers and sellers are normally represented by real estate agents. The agents will get together and have back-and-forth conversations.

Here is how it typically works:

> **Buyer:** Carl, I want that property, and I want to get it for a hundred grand. So, let us offer seventy.
>
> **Carl:** (buyer's broker) You know it is listed for a hundred and twenty, right? But I will present your seventy-thousand-dollar offer, but it may be too low to interest the seller.
>
> The seller's broker receives the seventy-thousand-dollar offer and puts in it to his seller.
>
> **Seller's broker:** That is ridiculous. The seller's property is at least worth one hundred and fifteen thousand. So, we will accept one hundred and fifteen thousand dollars.
>
> The seller's broker relays the counteroffer to Carl.
>
> Carl then sends the counteroffer to the buyer.

Buyer: I am not going to pay one hundred and fifteen thousand dollars. I will tell you what, I will bring my offer up ten thousand dollars and offer eighty thousand.

Every back and forth will cost the negotiators forty-eight to seventy-two hours because every contract comes with a clause giving forty-eight hours to the other party to respond or else the offer is no longer valid, and the contract is null and void.

So, what happens is that the buyer is back and forth with his lower offers engaging in the game called negotiating. Meanwhile, some other buyer sneaks in like a thief in the night. They talk to the seller's agent and do all the negotiating verbally and ends by snatching the property out from under the first buyer at whatever price is finally negotiated. Meanwhile, while the original deal is playing with the formal offers going back and forth—the deal is lost.

The lesson here is that you do not have time to approach negotiation in the traditional formal way in the high-stakes game of good deals.

Many people enjoy the game of negotiation, the act of driving down the price. There may be some who just love the game, seeing how well they can work the seller down to get the lowest price that they possibly can. The reality is you can avoid so much wasted time by getting into the negotiation process with your highest and best offer.

FIND THE PAYING POINTS

The best negotiating happens when you find the seller's paying points, and you offer up solutions. If you have not identified any of these points and you are saying, "Hey, I am an investor, and I want to buy your home. I am going to change this that and the other"—if that is your approach and you are going after the seller with that energy, no doubt you are going to turn him off even if he was motivated to sell. Maybe they are emotionally attached to the home or want their home sold to a good family. There are many reasons that you may not want to begin with that approach. So, you should first start a friendly conversation and find out what their needs are by asking the seller questions. You could simply begin by asking, "Why are you selling your home? Tell me your story." Then sit back and listen carefully to their issues.

Listening is one of the most important things you can do. In their enthusiasm, many investors talk over the seller and never hear what they have to say. They skip past this crucial element. Often by just listening, you can help the seller open up and provide actionable information you can use to make your best deal.

THE HIGHEST AND BEST

If you want to perform as an experienced real estate investor, just jump in with your best price. You say, "This is my price, and this is my best price." Highest and best mostly shows that you are a seasoned professional. You know what you are doing. You are not there to play around. Your aim when you put in your highest and best offer is for a twenty-four-hour turnaround time. When you approach a negotiation this way, it's "We are going to give you a real number here. We have done our numbers, and we know where we need to be."

Here is the benefit of this approach. If the seller comes back and refuses the offer, or they say they cannot come anywhere near the offer price, then you don't want to get stuck in that game any longer as you will not get the amount you need to receive to make your numbers work. You must move on and hunt the next deal that you want to do.

DO EVERYTHING VERBALLY FIRST

Negotiate all points verbally, so you are not caught in the detail of going back and forth. Have a real conversation before you put it to paper. If you are an investor working without a real estate agent, simply talk to the seller and outline your offer. Say something similar to: "This is what I am willing to put in. It is my highest and best. Is this something that is even in the realm of consideration?" If they say it is, then you have something to work with there. You would get after it and talk about it to solidify a deal. Such as, "I could go here, but I would need this much in closing costs, or I could go down here with a little less." You can do all of this verbally before you get into it and present the formal offer. So when you do, it will be accepted within the brief time window. Then you are done. You have the deal.

A good agent knows how to get behind closed doors and have a good conversation that says, "All right, let us be honest; let me tell you what my buyer wants for this. Where is your seller at? What are you guys able to do? Let us find out if we can make something happen."

All those pre-negotiations that happened verbally lead up to presenting a piece of paper that goes to the seller and gets approval right out of the gate, and we just skipped the entire game. Meanwhile, while everyone else is messing around trying to play the lowball offer game, we have an accepted offer.

INTRODUCING THE REAL ESTATE ESCALATION CLAUSE

Have you ever heard of an escalation clause? Seasoned real estate entrepreneurs have, and that is why they do more deals in hot markets than their competitors. The price escalation clause is one of the more excellent negotiating tools a buyer can pull out of his negotiation tool portfolio. This clause is perhaps the top contract addition that makes a contract attractive to a hesitant seller. But truthfully, you can be excused if you have never heard of the clause, and even some more experienced investors have not. As a result, many investors are ignorant as to what it can do for them.

Properly used, the escalation clause will make your offer the one that is the most appealing. It can be the most crucial factor in why your offer is accepted over all others. Here is why.

THE ESCALATION CLAUSE EXPLAINED

As the name implies, this paragraph is known as the escalation clause. When placed in a real estate contract, it allows the parties to the deal to increase their original offer. This clause provides the buyer insurance that higher offers will not outbid them if they are submitted later. This clause is not suitable for most transactions but can be a magic tool in certain instances.

Though it is written as a monetary clause, it is also enormously influential psychologically. It lets your seller know that you are deeply serious about the purchase and shows the extent to which you are willing to pursue the purchase. Of course, there is a condition as the clause will have a cap about how high over other bids it will go—another version uses a percentage rather than a dollar amount.

HOW DOES IT WORK?

The real estate escalation clause is straightforward. As the name implies, it allows an edge in the buyer's offer by giving the seller assurance that his prices will be the highest the buyer will receive, as the clause shows that the buyer will beat any future offer up to a certain amount. The way it works is the buyer's offer is accepted at $250,000 with his five-percent escalation clause. But later, the seller receives a second offer for $260,000. Without the escalation clause, the first buyer would lose the deal to the second buyer, who came in at $10,000 higher. However, since the first buyer agreed to pay a higher price than the original offer, up to five percent ($12,500), the first buyer would keep the deal. When using this method, you must be cautious to clarify exactly what the buyer is willing to pay over his original offer. Inserting such a clause will beat out other offers up to the buyer's limit.

WHEN TO USE THE CLAUSE

If you expect multiple offers to be made on investment property, that is the time to trot out the escalation clause. The clause is used as a competition reducer, assuring you of obtaining the deal's best chances. If your offer has an escalation clause, you can rest assured the seller will notice it. Of course, such a recommendation is only made when you, the buyer, are confident your numbers can support a higher price.

THE BENEFITS OF USING AN ESCALATION CLAUSE

There are many advantages to using an escalation clause. The first and foremost is that it increases your chances of a winning offer in a crowded field of bids. Your proposal will stay current during the bidding process rather than simply being eliminated when the first higher offer is received. You can remain in the active bidding process as you can increase your offer if required. The clause will most likely give you a winning outcome much of the time.

There are many other benefits that an escalation clause can provide if included in your real estate offers:

- The clause will lower the apprehension of a seller who may doubt his pricing.
- If correctly drafted, the clause can prevent a buyer from paying too much by escalating the price just enough without exceeding a predetermined amount.
- The escalation clause makes it a buyer's offer in that it favors the buyer, who uses it over any other buyer.
- Sellers take an offer with an escalation clause much more seriously, giving the advantage to anyone willing to include one.

ESCALATION CLAUSE DOWNSIDES

Adding an escalation clause has many benefits, but nothing is perfect. That remains true for this offering method as well. Earlier, we discussed keeping your numbers and wants to yourself and unknown to the buyer as it gives you more power in negotiations. But using the escalation clause requires you to reveal your top offer price. A good negotiator would tell you that is the wrong approach—do not identify what you are willing to spend; it removes your ability to negotiate a better price.

Equally important, in your haste to capture your deal, you can miscalculate your price ceiling. That would harm your cash flow and NOI.

- You may be accidentally spending more than you wanted to.
- It discloses the amount the investor is willing to pay.
- The escalation clause is a new idea which most investors and sellers may not be familiar with.
- Some sellers would be upset at your try to cut off legitimate offers.
- Sometimes the inclusion of an escalation clause might be an issue for the bank's appraiser.
- Despite the benefits, some sellers will not want such a clause in a contract.

THE STANDARD ESCALATION CLAUSE EXAMPLE

The language of the real estate escalation clause is fundamental. It must be clear, concise, and readily understood by both parties. The provision we are suggesting here is simple and straightforward. It is written to give you two alternatives. The first is a monetary amount. The second is a percentage. Use the one you are most comfortable with.

Here is what should be inserted in your offer as your escalation clause:

> *The buyer(s) hereby agrees that in the event the seller(s) receives a bona fide offer that exceeds the offer made herein, the buyer(s) will increase the offer price to $_____ above the amount of the original offer, but not to exceed $_____.*

> *Or*

> *_____percent above the amount of that offer, but not to exceed_____percent.*

You should have your attorney review this clause as contract laws vary from state to state. That is because some words carry more importance than others. As an example, the phrase 'bona fide offer' refers to when the initiation of the escalation clause should take effect. Otherwise, an illegitimate offer could be presented to increase your offer incorrectly.

SUMMARY

Negotiation is not a science. It is an art form to be studied. You must practice the excellent negotiation techniques listed here if you want more of your offers to be accepted. Understanding the basics of this art form is a must. Study the recommendations and know when to walk away from the closing table. Keep your information on maximum terms and price that you are willing to offer close to your chest. As you become more practiced with investment negotiation, you will be able to enter any deal with confidence and determination. Consider using the escalation clause in a competitive market as it will assure you more winning deals. Even as a beginning negotiator, you can become a successful dealmaker by following the simple rules of negotiation presented here.

THE NEXT STEP

Once the differences are worked out in the purchase contract, it is signed by both parties. Your escrow or earnest money deposit that you initially made is now turned over to the seller by the seller's attorney or escrow company.

These are the funds that ensured that you had "skin in the game" with the seller. They were held in a third-party account. The earnest money you advance in a purchase transaction is usually non-refundable, though your contract contingencies can sometimes give you a way out.

Your contract has most likely been negotiated to contain contingencies, such as inspection, loan approval, and a document review, which will now get underway.

With the signed purchase contract, off you go to present it to your lender for your formal mortgage application. The next chapter will take you through the financing steps to help you obtain the all-important mortgage commitment.

CHAPTER NINE

OBTAINING YOUR FINANCING

While I encourage people to save 100% down for a home, a mortgage is the one debt that I do not frown upon.

—Dave Ramsey

With all you learned so far, you should be itchy to buy that first investment property. So, what are your financing choices? A mortgage application is where the rubber meets the road as, when it comes to investment property financing, the first deal will be the hardest. That is because you are still learning, and you are now best to learn by experience. I assure you that your first purchase will result in significantly improved confidence. It will incentivize you so much that you will want to continue adding to your investment portfolio. This chapter will teach you about financing alternatives and how to buy that first property.

Your purchase price consists of two parts. The first part, the most substantial piece, is what you borrow. The second part of the equation is what you can put down. When you are beginning, there is usually a missing amount between those two figures. Either you cannot borrow enough as the property does not support it or you have inadequate funds of your own.

Traditional rental property loans usually need a minimum down payment. As you gain investment experience and build your wealth, these will be the types of loans you will seek. That is because they have competitive interest rates, and mortgage interest payments are tax-deductible on an investment property. They are an excellent alternative if you have good credit and plan to hold onto the property long-term as a rental. But as a novice investor, you will need to adopt different strategies to reduce the cash (cash you probably do not have) you put into a property.

How Mortgages Work

You are loaned a sum of money by a bank or mortgage company (typically 75 to 80 percent of the price of the property). You pay this loan back with interest using monthly payments over a set period, usually 25 to 30 years. If you do not repay the loan per the agreement, the property is forfeited through a legal process known as foreclosure.

Conventional Loan Down Payments

The purchase of a residential property with a traditional home loan typically requires that you must have a 20 percent down payment. But with a multi-family property, that number could be 25 percent or more. That is because commercial loans are unable to obtain mortgage insurance, so lenders need more of your equity in the deal to give themselves satisfactory protection against a possible default.

Besides more substantial down payments, your banker will want copies of the property's leases, two years of W-2 income, two years of tax returns, and evidence of savings. You will also need to provide several years of financial records if you are self-employed. The lender may even insist that your CPA prepare the financial statements. Last, but equally important, is your credit score. The credit score range that mortgage lenders use to approve a mortgage loan is 300 to 850, with an FHA loan needing at least 680.

There are differences between a bank and a credit union. A credit union can offer lower interest rates than traditional lenders, but it also has some limits on the use of proceeds. There are several differences between credit union loans and bank mortgages. The credit unions often offer:

- Lower interest rates and fees
- No private mortgage insurance requirement
- Easier application process
- A required membership
- Possible geographical limitations
- In 2017, credit unions issued 9% of all mortgages

WHO IS SUPPLYING THE MORTGAGE MONEY?

As recently as 2010, three banks (Wells Fargo, Bank of America, and Chase) originated 56 percent of all mortgages.[13] But in 2017, Wells Fargo, Bank of America, Chase, and all other banks put together originated just 40 percent of all loans.[1]

"Nonbank" lending, both credit unions and non-depository lenders have continued to cut into banks' share of the mortgage market. Also, 51 percent of all mortgages in 2017 came from non-depository lending institutions like Quicken Loans and PennyMac. Behind Wells Fargo ($212 billion) and Chase ($108 billion), Quicken ($86 billion) was the third-largest mortgage issuer in 2017. In the fourth quarter of 2017, PennyMac issued $17 billion in loans and was the fifth-largest lender overall.[1]

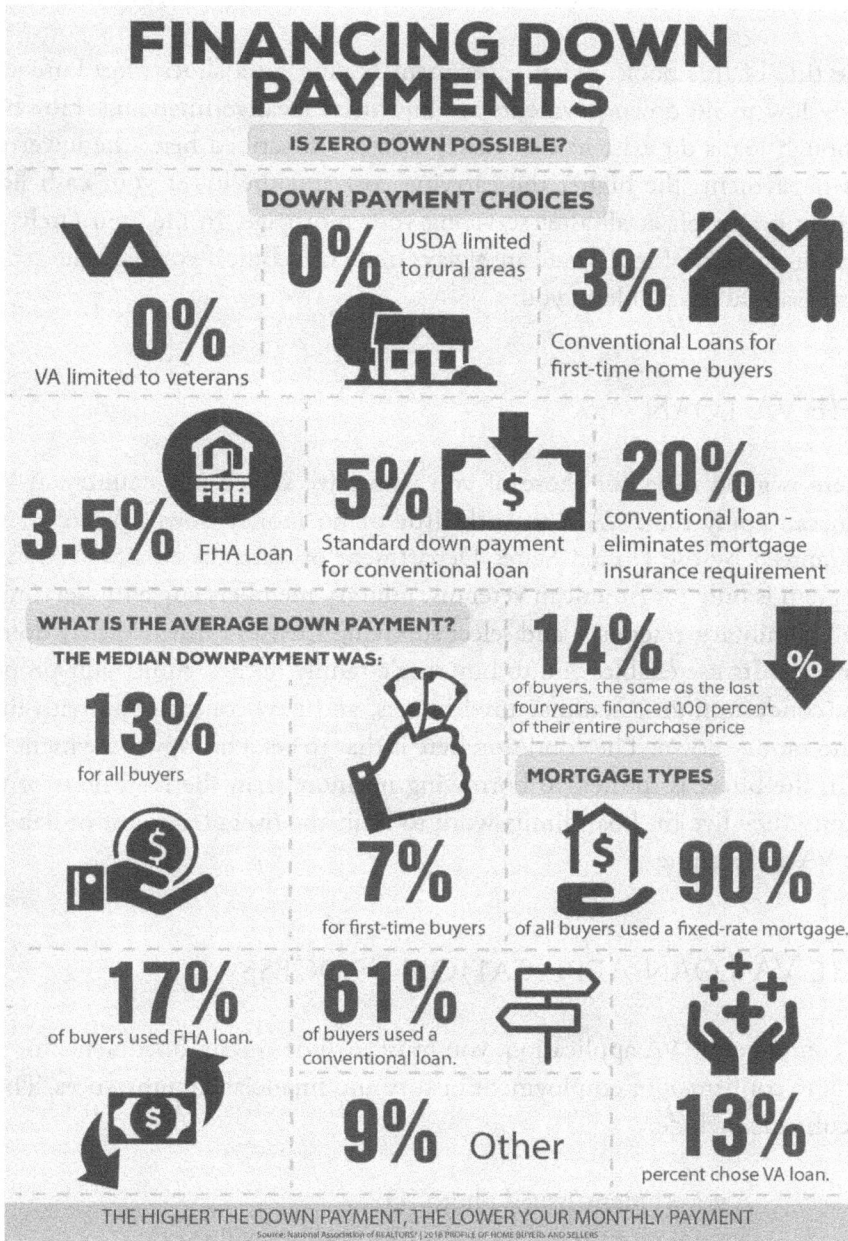

Figure 6. Mortgage financing choices.

Low- and No-Down-Payment Financing

The title of this book invites investment buying on a shoestring. Purchases using low to no down payments are known as creative financing. However, although loans do exist in the variety of types described here, the lower the down payment, the higher the carrying cost and the lower your cash flow, if there is any left at all after servicing your mortgage. In life, you rarely get something for nothing. There are always trade-offs. But, if you have the credit, these loans are available to you.

The VA Loan

There is good news for those of you who have served our country. A veteran can apply for a VA loan with little or no money down. A VA loan is guaranteed by the United States Department of Veterans Affairs (VA). The program is only for American veterans, military members currently serving in the US military, reservists, and select surviving spouses (provided they do not remarry). Its use enables you to buy single-family homes, multi-unit properties, condominiums, manufactured homes, and new construction with little or no money down. The condition here is that to get a no-down-payment VA loan, the buyer is limited to borrowing no more than the loan limit of the county they live in. Loan limits work to limit the overall amount of liability the VA will assume.

The VA Loan Application Process

To complete the VA application, you must include certain documents for the bank to confirm your employment history and financial circumstances. These documents include:

- A government-issued photo ID
- Several months of pay stubs (the number will vary)
- Two to three years' worth of W-2 statements
- Bank account, investment, and 401(k) monthly statements

- If you have self-employment, 1099, or rental income, the last two years of federal tax returns
- Copy of your DD-214. It is proof of your military service. It gives the details of your discharge, dates of service, and current classification
- If you are on active military duty, a statement of service letter signed by your commanding officer

You may be required to provide supporting information depending on your circumstances. The motivation of the VA is to approve of your application. They will help a fellow service member to receive their stamp of approval.

It is essential to fill out your VA credit application as accurately as you can, as it will be scrutinized and verified. Omitting negative or positive information will delay the credit review process and often leads to rejection.

The VA will then determine your eligibility and, if you are qualified, the VA will issue you a Certificate of Eligibility that you need to submit for a VA loan.

How to Apply for a VA Loan

To obtain a Certificate of Eligibility, you must meet one of the following criteria:

- Ninety days of consecutive active service during wartime
- One hundred eighty-one days of active service during peacetime
- At least six years' service in the National Guard or Reserves
- Be a spouse of a service member who has died in the line of duty
- Be a spouse of a service member who has died because of a service-related disability

The Certificate of Eligibility (COE)

The COE affirms to lenders that you meet all requirements for the VA home credit advantage. The following method is how you can apply for a COE:

- Apply through your loan representative (most lenders will be able to get your COE for you).
- Apply on the web (through eBenefits.va.gov).
- Apply via mail (Complete VA Form 26-1880 and mail to VA Atlanta Regional Loan Center, Attn: COE (262), PO Box 100034, Decatur, GA 30031).

The Certificate of Eligibility (COE) does not guarantee a VA loan. The veteran must still have approvals from a lender for the mortgage loan from an income and credit standpoint. To be qualified, you must have acceptable credit and satisfactory pay, as well as a Certificate of Eligibility (COE). The home must be for your occupancy, but it can be multi-family. So, you can live in one side while your tenant or tenants help pay your mortgage. That is an excellent opportunity to be an investor and own your first multi-family with little or no cash outlay.

Of course, a VA mortgage is not the answer for every new multi-unit investor as not everyone has served our country. There are alternate programs available to investment purchases with limited funds.

OTHER PURCHASING METHODS USING LITTLE OR NO MONEY DOWN

Besides the VA loan, here are the nine ways to fund your real estate investing career when cash is tight:

1. **Navy Federal Credit Union.** The Navy Federal can offer a zero-percent-down mortgage option for military members, military families, and some civilian employees of the US Department of Defense.

You can get approved for a mortgage without a down payment, and you will have to pay a fee. However, that funding fee is often lower than the VA loan funding fee, depending on your situation.

But even if you are not a veteran, do not be disappointed. There are many opportunities for you, too. There are no-money-down programs available to non-veterans as well. So, anyone can get started with little or no savings in the bank. It is just a matter of a bit more effort. But you can do it.

2. **Use the USDA No Money Down Multi-Family Program.** You can invest in your first multi-family property to live in with a zero down payment using the USDA loan program. A USDA loan is a zero-down-payment mortgage. Eligible homebuyers located in rural and suburban areas can get this financing through the USDA loan program. The program is administered through the United States Department of Agriculture (USDA). This department backs various loans to help low- or moderate-income people buy, repair, or renovate a home in a rural area. Eligible buyers gain several advantages, such as 100% financing with no down payment and below-market mortgage rates.

This program provides competitive funding for affordable multi-family rental housing for low-income, elderly, or disabled individuals and families in eligible rural areas. The USDA program was established for qualified applicants that cannot obtain commercial credit that would allow the borrowers to charge rents affordable to low-income tenants. Qualified applicants include individuals, trusts, associations, partnerships, limited partnerships, nonprofit organizations, for-profit corporations, and consumer cooperatives. Also, it helps most state and local governmental entities as well as federally recognized Tribes.

You must live in your property for a minimum of one year. But then you can move out to convert your property fully to a multi-family rental while you search for your next investment. Living in your investment properties is an excellent way to avoid the stricter lender rules for investment properties.

Qualifying for a Nothing-Down USDA Loan.

To qualify for a USDA loan, your income cannot exceed 115 percent of the median income for the location of your property. You must have a good credit history and qualify to afford the mortgage payments, taxes, and insurance for the property. These are low-interest 30-year loans. USDA also offers single-home financing. Their down payment and credit score requirements for a primary residence are less strict than for investment property. So, if you run into that issue, look to a single-family home as your first investment.

State housing agencies issue these loans throughout the United States. If you are excited to get involved, contact your local state RD Office for details and current interest rates applicable to your proposed property purchase. Though it is an excellent program, loan applications are limited to submittal just once a year. Check the Federal Register for the Notice of Funding Availability (NOFA).

For more information, visit the USDA home page at https://eligibility. sc.egov.usda.gov/eligibility/welcomeAction.do.

3. FHA Loan Low Down Duplex Financing. Another government loan program enables you to finance a two-unit duplex. As of March 2015, the down payment requirement for an owner-occupied duplex was only 3.5 percent. Which means you must occupy one of the units. The second unit will pay much of your mortgage. Later, you can move and rent the second unit so you can have a fully tenanted duplex. If, for example, your new duplex is selling for $300,000, you would need $10,500 to put down. You might borrow this from family, add to credit cards, or ask the seller to hold a small 3 to 5-year purchase money mortgage.

Qualifications for an FHA Loan

FHA Loans have less rigorous credit requirements compared to a conventional loan. But you must be able to qualify for most of the FHA loan requirements to receive approval. If you fail one of its required standards, you still may be approved by providing a satisfactory explanation.

You will need to provide two years of W-2s to prove two years of constant employment in the same line of work and that your income has remained the same or increased.

The qualified credit score must be 620 or higher with less than two 30-day-late payments in the past 12 months, one 60-day-late payment and any other delayed payment in the last 12 months, or one 90-day-late payment in the previous 12 months.

Some lenders will accept a lower credit score (as low as 500) with a down payment of only 10 percent. As an alternative, a credit score of 580 with 3.5 percent down will be enough.

A bankruptcy discharge date cannot be within two years of the FHA case assignment date, or there must have been no foreclosure in the past three years. You must intend to live in the property you're buying. But you can purchase a multi-family if you will reside in one of the units.

Of course, you must also have a 3.5 percent cash down payment on your loan.

4. Home Possible Advantage program one percent down. Use a lender that either pays closing costs or offers a rebate on your down payment. With Freddie Mac's Home Possible Advantage program, Quicken Loans has a 1 percent down payment option on single-family primary residences for owner-occupied properties. The buyer puts up 1 percent, and Quicken Loans provides a grant for the other 2 percent needed. A 680-credit score and a debt-to-income ratio of 45 percent or less are required. It will allow you to purchase a single-family residence to build equity. In the future, as the property appreciates, you can refinance and take out investment capital tax-free.

5. Use the seller carry-back technique. Many have never heard of the term 'seller carry-back,' yet it can resolve many financing problems and cash shortfalls if you understand this investment strategy.

The technique is also known as seller financing or "owner will carry" (OWC). It is a useful real estate tool for both the seller and the buyer. The appeal for seller financing or owner carries mortgages is growing today. Unlike during the 70s and 80s, when interest rates were in the double digits, it has gained popularity recently because of rapidly increasing property values and the capital-gains rules.

According to the National Association of Realtors, about 40 percent of all home sales in 1981 used seller financing. That was because then, the average 30-year fixed-rate mortgage reached an interest rate of 18.63 percent.

Currently, that percentage is hovering around 4 percent because of low interest and the fact that most buyers can qualify for traditional loans.

But there is a renewed appeal, brought on by soaring real estate appreciation and an Internal Revenue Service rule that limits tax-free home-sales profits to $250,000 for an individual or $500,000 a couple filing joint returns. Beyond that, it is subject to up to 15 percent in federal taxes.

When selling your primary home, you can make up to $250,000 in profit or double that if you are married, and you won't owe anything for capital gains. You must pay capital gains tax on a home sale if you are over the limit.

With the change in IRS rules, owners are discovering that when they sell, they will exceed the tax-free capital-gains ceiling. However, the best way to avoid the extra tax load is for the seller to hold the mortgage on the property.

As the buyer, you should explain all the benefits of holding the mortgage to your potential seller. As mentioned above, it is a way of avoiding capital gains taxes on excess gain on a sale. The seller could accept a higher interest rate, which would provide a higher monthly income than the seller could get from a bank or CD. The mortgage could be limited to a shorter term, such as five years (this is known as a balloon mortgage).

It is an excellent alternative for buyers who do not qualify for conventional loans. This technique is not only for the novice investor but is useful for the experienced investor, too. For example, if a buyer-investor owns several investment properties, the interest rate on a conventional mortgage would be higher than the current market on a traditional loan, and the buyer may have to get a portfolio loan.

Portfolio mortgages are more expensive as they are loans originated by a lender and then held—kept in the lender's portfolio—for the life of the loan. It makes them different from most mortgages, which are unsalable on the secondary mortgage market.

Buying a house where the seller holds the mortgage allows you to agree on a reasonable interest rate without the need to take out another loan for this investment property.

This financing method is a bit more challenging to get, as you must sell it to the seller. But there are many advantages to the seller, and it can be hugely favorable to you if you can achieve it. But it is up to you to explain it to them.

A great benefit of owner financing is the monthly income it provides to the seller. Offering to hold a mortgage as a seller can be a great way to make money with above-market interest rates.

By creating a winning solution for you and your buyer, you will obtain a more competitive price for your home and earn extra money by collecting interest as part of the loan.

The way it works is the seller accepts a down payment that you both agree on. The seller then receives a monthly payment of principal and interest from the buyer.

This approach works best with sellers who are mortgage-free. It provides them a source of income with a higher interest rate than that they could get elsewhere.

Sellers negotiate the terms of the loan and interest rate with the buyer. Often the loan is for a shorter term such as five or ten years, with a balloon payment due at the end of the term.

If the buyer does not pay, the seller has recourse to take back his property. The ability to foreclose on the property means the seller can take the property back if the buyer defaults on payments. In turn, the seller gets to keep all the money the buyer has paid to date.

6. Use a Home Equity Line of Credit (HELOC). Taking out a line of credit on your home (a HELOC) or another property you may own enables you to find the cash to use for real estate investing. With a home equity loan, you can establish a line of credit for 70 to 80 percent of the equity in your property. To use a simple example, say your home appraises at $300,000, but your mortgage balance is $100,000. That means you have $200,000 equity available. Eighty percent of that (0.80 x 200,000) equals a possible home equity loan of $160,000.

You can use this money for a down payment on an investment rental property. By receiving a traditional 75 percent mortgage and using proceeds from your HELOC, you will complete your purchase financing like a zero-down transaction as it is all borrowed funds.

The cost of a home equity loan is typically the prime rate plus one to two percent; as of this writing, the prime rate is 3.25 percent, so the cost would be about 5.25 percent. It is a bit higher than the traditional 30-year mortgage but has the added advantage of lower ancillary costs. With a HELOC, there are no closing costs. Plus, you have the added benefit of a quick closing, as the appraisal is often just a drive-by. Often there is not even a charge for the assessment.

Using your credit line to pay for the rental property allows you to use the rent to pay down the HELOC every month. You can determine how much you wish to pay every month toward the principal. Since a HELOC is usually a variable-rate loan, you would want to pay off the principal as rapidly as possible while interest rates remain low. If the prime rate remains stable, the interest owed each month is reduced.

7. Ask the seller to pay closing costs. On some real estate transactions, the property seller offers to pay buyer closing costs to incentivize a sale. However, the tradeoff is you will probably have to provide the full asking price or close to it. It is reasonable if your rent is enough to cover all your expenses and give you some cash flow. But the danger is that if your lender quotes a mortgage payment (including taxes and insurance) that is higher than the rent you can charge, you will run a loss. Investment properties must have a positive cash flow to cover vacancies and repairs.

8. Conventional 97 mortgages. The Conventional 97 mortgage is a loan that allows you to have a loan-to-value (LTV) ratio of as high as 97 percent. For example, if you are buying a home with a $200,000 asking price, you can borrow up to $194,000 and have just $6,000 to put down as your down payment.

The mortgage is available from Fannie Mae and Freddie Mac, and though a Conventional 97 requires only a 3 percent down payment, you will still be required to pay monthly mortgage insurance. However, an advantage of this mortgage is the down payment may come from gifts. As a result, you can get help from close relatives in raising the money to make your down payment.

The Conventional 97 mortgage is similar in terms of most traditional loans. A breakdown of the program's highlights includes:

- Loan limits: Loan amount must not exceed the conforming limit for the county in which the property is located
- Loan type: A fixed-rate mortgage with a term not exceeding 30 years
- Property type and eligibility: Must be owner-occupied. Investment properties are excluded as the loan must be for:
    o Single-unit family home
    o Cooperative
    o Condominium
    o Planned unit development (PUD)
- Mortgage Insurance: Borrowers must pay private mortgage insurance (PMI). It is a standard requirement for conventional loans with an LTV of 80 percent or higher. However, PMI can be requested to be removed once the borrower's LTV reaches 78 percent
- Down payment: Not less than 3 percent of the purchase price. No minimum contribution from the borrower needed. Payment can be from gifted funds. But down payments sourced from a gift may raise the credit requirement for the loan

Conventional 97 Mortgage Qualifications

Borrowers must meet the following requirements:

- A credit score of 620 or higher
- One borrower must qualify as a first-time homebuyer
- Must not have owned a home within three years

- No more than a 43-percent debt-to-income ratio (DTI)

Additionally, Conventional 97 loans have no income limit, which is another excellent trait that sets them apart from other low-down-payment loan options.

9. Private money. These are lenders that have the funds available to finance a real estate investment—and more importantly—who would be willing to secure a loan on your property with the title or deed to your investment property in exchange for returns, since many investors do not have enough money in the bank to pay cash. And hard money loans are expensive, often wiping out all a deal's profit. Private money loans come from wealthy individuals. It is just like borrowing hard money, except:

- the interest rates are typically much lower,
- there are usually few or no fees, and
- the private lenders are typically much easier to work with!

Most investors do not use private money for a straightforward reason. They do not know a private money lender, so they do not have access to their funds! A search on Google will find many private money lenders available to discuss your investment plans.

THE RISKS OF OVER-BORROWING

When properly used, real estate leverage (the amount borrowed versus the amount you invested in a purchase) can be used to increase return on investment. The key is to avoid deciding without proper consideration of the areas of risk in leverage. Avoid these high-risk behaviors, and you have a far better chance of realizing success in using real estate leverage.

This chapter has shown you the many ways you can buy with little or none of your own money invested. While that solves one problem—lack of investment capital—it sets up significant risk which you need to be aware of. Using leverage in real estate investing is a smart thing to do to build returns. To mitigate such risks, you must be mindful of and avoid the following mistakes:

Do not rely on high appreciation. Over the long haul, real estate values prove themselves to increase. The risk you face is that it is cyclic in the short term in that values may not increase over a one-to-five-year cycle. Investors often overlook this trap when the market is surging, and real estate is rapidly appreciating. You cannot count on such highs from one year to the next. Inevitably, there will be a dip. You need to be financially positioned to wait out the pause. Never, never expect continued high appreciation as it will lead you to overpay. A year or two of deflation can cause a property to lose value and put you in financial jeopardy.

Runaway from high financing payments. If you are investing with little or nothing down, you must buy a property that is under-market priced. It is up to you and not your lender to find out what you can afford. For example, you may qualify for that investment property. An FHA lender may likely commit to a 3.5-percent-down mortgage to allow you to buy a $450,000 investment property. But you must add the monthly cost of paying for financing by creating an NOI and cash flow budget. There is no shame in turning down the financing if there is little or no bottom line to service an emergency, such as a long-term vacancy. Go back to the seller and negotiate the price down, explaining the property is not financeable at his current price. If you cannot make your monthly mortgage payments because you were too hasty to accept excessive financing, you risk foreclosure, but worse, you risk ruining your credit rating for many years. It will put you out of the real estate investment business for a long while. And you are tarnishing your credit for years to come.

Avoid bad investments. Yes, you are correct. This book is about investing and focusing on little or no money down. But just because you can occasionally does mean it is advisable. In certain situations, it is wise to buy a prized property using a bit more equity. If you do not have cash available, then look for a partner (not a lender) to help with the purchase. Adding cash now gives you the ability to pay, leaving you with a cash cushion for things that can go wrong. Added money may also enable you to be eligible for a lower interest rate, avoiding private insurance fees. Sometimes leverage is tempting and sensible, while other times it can be filled with risk. You must decide what is best for you.

HOW TO USE LEVERAGE WISELY

To be a successful investor, you must learn to use leverage strategically. A good investor is continuously on the lookout for investment opportunities, not only the right property but the right economic conditions. After detailed due diligence reveals flaws, the best investors turn down deals, and you must also be ready to walk away from deals that don't meet your stringent requirements. You, too, must ensure that you conduct proper due diligence to prevent a severe financial misstep.

Due diligence. The care that a reasonable person takes to avoid harming other persons or their property is known as due diligence. For investment property due diligence, the Forbes Real Estate Council encourages investors to ask questions like,

"How have property values trended in the area? What known factors, like the arrival or departure of a major employer, will influence the economy in the months, years, and decades ahead? What are the expectations for the broader regional and national economy for the foreseeable future?"

The answers to these and related questions are critical.

Investment strategy. You need to set up your investment guidelines. Now that you are thinking about buying your first investment property, you must decide if it will be held for the short or long-term, as that makes a difference in your approach and how you will operate the property. This answer allows you to set up several rules about when you exit the investment and when you wait it out. You do not need to stop and think when the market begins to change along these lines. Use sound judgment: if you feel that you are taking on too much risk with excessively small potential for reward, exit. Real estate investment always comes with risk. You must decide how much you can accept to sleep at night.

You must decide how you want real estate investing to guide your long-term personal objectives. Regardless of whether you get a zero-down property loan, have the cash to provide the traditional 20-percent down payment, or do something in between, consider your situation and make a choice that's right for your risk tolerance.

HOW TO MAKE A MORTGAGE LOAN APPLICATION

Now that you know how mortgages work, what must you do to apply for one, and how do you obtain your best chances for approval?

As we discussed in an earlier chapter, the next thing you should get after finding an investor-savvy real estate agent is a mortgage pre-approval letter. You will need this so the seller and your agent will know you can finance the offers you make and take you seriously.

ALPHA BAY BANK
Your Community Bank

Roberta Adams
Senior Loan Officer
EX 235

CREDIT APPROVAL

5674 Ellsworth Avenue
Alpha Bay, WI **54302**
1-800-ALPHABAY

Date: May 26, 2019

To: Charles J. and Dorothy Dutton
Address: Property Address
Rancho Cordova, CA 95670

Please be advised that based on the information provided. we have determined that the above-mentioned individuals are credit approved for a mortgage with the following terms:

Sale Price: $280.500
Loan Amount: $270.682
Loan Type: FHA
Loan Term: 30 year
LTV: 96.5%

Conditions of credit approval to be submitted for final loan commitment:

1. W2 statements tor previous two years
2. Tax returns (for previous two years)
3. Pay stubs for all borrowers, previous thirty days period (all Jobs)
4. Bank Statements — ALL PAGES- previous two months
5. 401k Statement — ALL Pages
6. Copy of Driver's License and Social Security Card
7. Borrower to provide policy of fire and hazard insurance prior to close of escrow

(Note: This letter in neither a loan commitment nor a combination of a lock-in of any interest rate.)

This credit approval is based upon an application, credit report, and supporting documentation supplied to us by the individual(s) and is therefore subject to approval of all information provided and the receipt of such additional information customarily requested by Alpha Bay Bank in the processing of applications for this type of loan. This approval is based upon the property being occupied as a primary residence, *Changes in your income, assets, or liabilities may void this credit approval and or require the approval to be reconsidered.* A full loan commitment can only be issued upon full current evaluation and acceptance of the property as well as the applicants' ability to fulfill all underwriting conditions including investor approval. it necessary.

If you have any questions, please do not hesitate to give me a call

Respectfully,

Roberta Adams
Senior Loan Officer

Figure 7. Example of pre-approval letter. Format will vary between lenders.

WHAT IS A PRE-APPROVAL LETTER?

As you begin the process of applying for a mortgage, you will hear two terms used almost interchangeably—pre-approval and pre-qualification. They both refer to lender letters which show the lenders feel that you have the resources to qualify for a mortgage loan. But they are different.

The mortgage pre-approval/qualification letter is an important document issued by a lender which lists the loan amount they are willing to make to you. It is not yet a guarantee, as is given in the commitment letter after the bank reviews added documents including the contract to buy a property. However, the message does hold significant weight in the eyes of a seller and your real estate agent.

MORTGAGE PRE-APPROVAL AND PREQUALIFICATION

Research different lenders. Paying off a mortgage can take up to thirty years. You will want to verify both the lender's and loan servicer's trustworthiness. You should make it a habit to check out both lender and servicer (if different from the lender; make sure you ask the lender who is servicing the loan) on the complaint database of the Consumer Financial Protection Bureau at https://www.consumerfinance.gov/data-research/consumer-complaints/ and with the Better Business Bureau.

Apply for credit approval and compare offers. Next, after you have used your pre-qualifications to narrow down your lender choices to the few with the best rates and fees, you start to apply for pre-approval. Once you have a few pre-approvals, you can often use them to negotiate better terms with lenders.

Before filling out the mortgage application, you should take your pre-approval letter from one lender and show it to another and ask them if they can do better. Just a slight difference in the interest rate will make a big difference in the cost over the life of your mortgage.

Avoid the "hard credit pull." Each time there is an inquiry to the credit bureaus, it counts as a hard pull. It lowers your credit score a few points. Lenders will check your credit during the pre-approval process. But if you are shopping around and multiple lenders check your credit over a 45-day window, the credit bureaus will count these inquiries as a single credit pull.

How to Improve Your Chances
of Getting Preapproved

Before applying to any lender, you should know about your creditworthiness in advance. There are several ways to give yourself a credit polish to make sure your application is approved. For example, if you have the income, but see something on your credit report that a lender might question, resolve that first before making an application that will be rejected.

Fix errors on your credit report. Since nothing in life is perfect, especially credit reports, you want to scour yours for mistakes. Look for wrong identification information; data about someone else entirely; signs of identity fraud, such as accounts you did not open; account status errors; and improper payment and balance information. If you find such errors, contact the credit bureau and dispute them.

Pay down your debt. Your credit score is calculated using several parameters. The important ones consist of payment history and the debt you amassed. You can figure this out by using an online credit score simulator like the one located here: https://www.creditkarma.com/tools/credit-score-simulator. It will show you how much your score will improve if you pay down your debts. It is a useful tool.

Build your savings account. The more money in your savings account, the better you are as a candidate for lending. Even your 401(k) savings will benefit you in the loan underwriting process. Try to stash away three months' worth of mortgage payments to help for financial emergencies. If you have six months' worth, it is even better in the review process. That will aid you in keeping your mortgage current during a difficult time, as it is hard to catch up from falling behind on your mortgage. Besides, the banks add late fees, interest, and penalties.

The Borrower Approval Process

There are usually three approval steps that you will go through during your banking lending experience. Each approval or qualification places you one step closer to your property purchase.

Pre-qualification. Though this step does not carry significant weight, it is helpful to new borrowers to see where their credit stacks up in the eyes of a potential lender. At this stage, a lender gives a glimpse of your financial situation. The lender will calculate your debt to income ratio (DTI) and inquire about your income and debts. Before you meet with the loan officer, you should already have checked your credit. It is essential, for if a loan officer must pull your credit, it will lower your credit score. Tell your loan officer about your credit so he does not have to check it further. Your credit report will be pulled later, just not now. This pre-qualification is only for informational purposes between you and your lender. The real estate broker will expect you to produce a pre-approval letter before they work with you.

The primary reason you will want to prequalify when shopping for mortgage lenders is to get an idea of the lender's interest rates and other terms.

QUESTIONS TO ASK YOUR LENDER

These are some of the questions you need to ask your lender while discussing your pre-qualification letter:

- Based on our goals, what loan alternatives do you recommend?
- What is your current interest rate?
- Do you offer rate locks? If so, how does it work?
- What are points, and are they in my home loan quote?
- What are my all-in costs?
- Does my loan have pre-payment penalties?
- Where does the underwriting process occur?
- How long does it take you to close on my loan?
- What is your successful closing ratio?
- After my loan closes, is it sold?
- Who services my loan?

Pre-approval. A mortgage pre-approval is what you need to make offers. A pre-approval letter is considered the minimum qualification a home buyer needs to shop for properties. That is because, at this junction, the letter represents that your credit and income have been verified. The verification process begins with the lender needing the document types listed below:

A credit report that shows the borrower's FICO score and credit history

A loan application (The standard Fannie Mae 1003; see Addendum) is filled out and put into a loan file. The following documents are required:

- Borrower identification (e.g., driver's license)
- W-2s (2 years)
- Recent pay stubs (30 days)
- Recent bank statements (2 months)
- Current assets (retirement accounts)

After you have provided these documents, the bank's underwriter will review them and make a positive or negative decision. If it is approved, the underwriter will issue the bank's pre-approval letter. The underwriter has confirmed all your information, which makes the pre-approval letter more meaningful.

The pre-approval letter usually includes essential information such as the loan amount, the loan type, and ofttimes an average of monthly mortgage payment (see Table 7, Alpha Bay Bank example) with an estimate of your loan amount, the interest rate, and the monthly mortgage payment. The pre-approval gives you an advantage over buyers who do not have one, and it is still not a commitment from the bank. However, the benefit is that it does not commit you to that bank's mortgage. You can use the pre-approval letter for about 30 to 60 days.

WHY IS THE PRE-APPROVAL LETTER SO IMPORTANT?

When you have received your pre-approval letter, that means you have your financing source in place, and you are ready and able to buy a home in confidence. The pre-approval letter is proof the lender has studied your credit and finances and that all parties involved can be confident the transaction can go forward once your offer is accepted.

With a pre-approval letter, you are in a better negotiating position as sellers know that your offer is serious and should be considered. It is an important competitive position, especially if other potential buyers do not have pre-approval from their lender. Smart sellers are going to take the path of least resistance. With your pre-approval, you are in the best position to get the deal done.

LENDER COMMITMENT LETTER

The lender commitment letter is the final step in getting a mortgage. The lender's underwriter completes the last review on your file. The appraiser and title company also complete their work. The lender approves your loan with listed conditions to be satisfied.

You are now able to provide a copy of the mortgage commitment letter to your seller. Presenting the mortgage commitment letter to the seller should also halt any other parties interested in the property. Once your seller accepts your offer, you tell the lender, so the loan file goes through the final underwriting and is cleared to close. The last step is then the closing, where the buyer and seller meet at the title company's or the bank's attorney's office to complete document signing and to exchange funds.

GETTING A MORTGAGE WHEN YOU'RE SELF-EMPLOYED

A lender's underwriter has a more difficult time in the mortgage approval process if you are a self-employed individual. Lenders are not only examining your credit but that of your business. Because of that issue, as a policy, some lenders will not lend to self-employed applicants.

Lenders need reassurance that their loans can be repaid. They will want proof that your income is not only high enough but historically consistent. They also want to see that you have a good track record of repaying your debts.

It translates to more documents, tax returns, and evidence of payments to your company. They will also want to review supporting business operations, such as an existing business website.

The challenge here to getting a mortgage is proving a consistent and increasing income. Lenders will want to see at least two years of self-employment income to qualify you for a mortgage.

What Is a Letter of Explanation?

A lender will want an explanation if your credit report has any adverse remarks. They usually will not reject a mortgage application. Instead, they will seek a letter of explanation. Receiving a letter request is nothing to be upset about; consider it your opportunity to tell your story and explain any negative remarks in your credit report. The letter request provides the mortgage lender a better understanding of your financial situation and anything else that has damaged your credit score.

Letter of Explanation

Understand the whole purpose of a lender's review of your credit report is to verify there is nothing negative that could affect the repayment of its loan by you. If an item is found, such as a late payment, delinquency, charge-off, bankruptcy, foreclosure, or judgment, they want to better understand the extenuating circumstances involved.

If you are applying for a government-backed home loan through the Federal Housing Administration loan programs or the US Department of Agriculture loan programs, the lender you are using is required by these agencies to take special care in checking your credit history. Those loan programs require this for underwriting. Just as with a conventional mortgage, if your credit report potentially hurts your ability to qualify for a government-backed mortgage, a letter of explanation will be required. This requirement applies to an application for a conventional, jumbo mortgage (a jumbo mortgage is one over $453,100 to $721,050) or a refinance home loan that is not from a government loan program.

The explanation letter makes getting approved for a mortgage more frustrating, but it is a good signal. The letter of explanation allows you to provide added information that could convince them to approve your application.

WHEN A LETTER OF EXPLANATION MAY BE REQUIRED

A letter of explanation might be requested if anything in your credit history or financial situation is determined to be questionable during underwriting.

If you have pulled your credit history in advance, as is strongly recommended, none of it should be a surprise. The lender will want you to explain accounts in collections, excess late payments, and of course, judgments or bankruptcies.

An explanation may be required for something as mundane as the name and address on your credit report not matching your mortgage application's name and address.

The are other reasons the lender may ask for explanations besides questions on your credit report. Questions could arise while examining your bank statements. Large deposits, overdrafts, and account transfers may cause questions. Your work history might trigger questions about such things as income swings, many job changes, or periods of unemployment.

SAMPLE LETTER OF EXPLANATION

If your lender requests a letter of explanation, you will need to know what you should include. Of course, you do not need to guess; ask the lender for the specific questions they would like answered. However, having an example of a letter of explanation is helpful. So, we have provided one below. Make it brief, but not so short that your answer needs further explanation.

Here is a letter of explanation sample for a late payment inconsistency:

Dear Ladies and Gentlemen:

Thank you for your inquiry to explain a question on my credit report. The recent late payment reported for my March car payment was a misunderstanding. My wife and I were visiting her sister, who had just had a baby. In our rush and our excitement to see our new niece, we had forgotten to drop the payment in the mail when we left. Since we pride ourselves on prompt payment as our credit history supports,

you can imagine our embarrassment when we arrived home
and found the unsent envelope on the kitchen counter. We
called Ford Motor Company to explain. However, even
though it was received one day after its grace period, we were
dinged with a late payment report.

Best regards,

(Name)

Your letter should be clear and include what the lender asks for. Do not go overboard with information. Be truthful but slant your letter to the favorable side to sway the lender into overlooking the issues that they were concerned about.

SUMMARY

This chapter has covered the various types of mortgages that you might consider using to buy your first investment property. We have shown how to apply for them and how to give yourself the best chances for approval. If you have not done so already, get your pre-approval letter from your local lender. It is an essential step in your investment acquisition plan.

NEXT STEPS

In the next chapter, we will discuss due diligence and the importance of property inspections, the final steps before you close on your new acquisition. Please read on.

CHAPTER TEN

DUE DILIGENCE
INSPECTIONS

Buyers decided in the first eight seconds of seeing a home if they are interested in buying it. Get out of your car, walk in their shoes, and see what they see.

—Barbara Corcoran

Years ago, I nervously bought my second investment property. It was three units consisting of a duplex and a small two-bedroom cottage located on a quiet residential street on the outskirts of the Hamptons on Long Island. It was the perfect affordable summer rental. I quickly filled it with groups of flight attendants from New York City, who leased all three units for the summer. It was a sweet setup and though older, it had no maintenance issues. After the leases were signed, I looked forward to a grand summer. That is until I received a call three weeks later from a neighbor who was complaining about weekend party noise. The complaint started an unwanted chain of events. Shortly after that, I received a registered "cease" letter from code enforcement telling me the property was an illegal multi-family. I must bring it into conformance within thirty days. I was stunned. I thought I was careful as I had used a local attorney for the purchase. I had title insurance, too, yet as it turned out, no one had visited or checked with the town before the purchase to verify zoning and the property's conforming use. That should have been one of the first inspections to make. I blame myself. It was an expensive lesson for me as a novice investor, a disastrous due diligence failure. Through some quick negotiation, I was able to save the summer. However, in the fall, I was forced to sell the property after owning it for only eleven months. Sloppy due diligence can and will burn an investor. I know to this day that I still kick myself for having to give up such a profit-making setup.

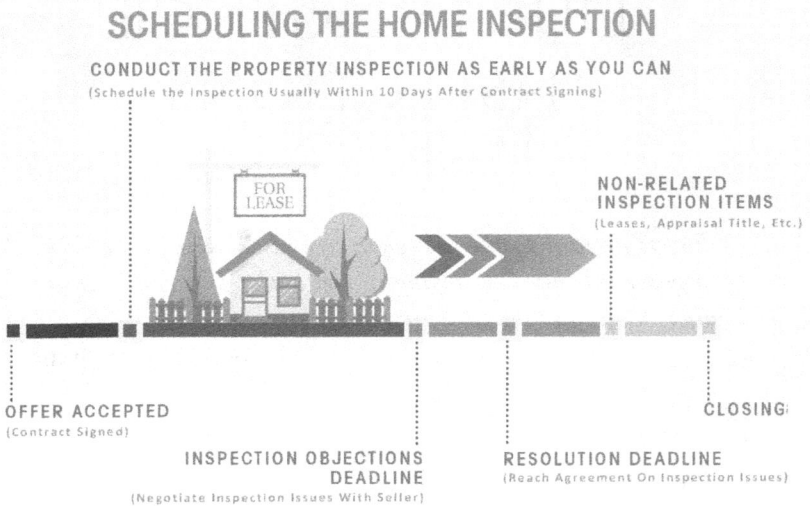

Figure 8. Leave as much time as possible between your inspection and your inspection objection deadline.

WHAT IS DUE DILIGENCE?

The more formal definition of due diligence is a comprehensive review of a real property conducted by a prospective buyer or his agents to find out its condition and if it is a residential rental or commercial property, to evaluate its financial potential. The chief aims of real estate due diligence are to thoroughly inspect the fundamentals of the property, seller, financing, and compliance duties to reduce and mitigate financial uncertainties.

The due diligence of a real estate transaction is a critical part of the purchasing process as it provides the buyer the opportunity to have the home professionally inspected, formally investigate the neighborhood, and work with his lender. Many think of it as a mere home inspection, and in part, it is. But it is much more than that. It begins with your initial analysis, even before you submit an offer. For example, your visits to the property and the neighborhood are fundamental to your evaluation and would be considered informal due diligence as, if things look useful to you, it encourages you to proceed with a possible transaction.

Your act of reviewing a listing and confirming its cash flow potential is the first stage of informal due diligence. All these fact-finding activities are part of your due diligence. It may be considered informal due diligence as once the contract is signed; it will contain conditions that can only be verified through various inspections. That is the formal due diligence phase.

One of the advantages of conducting a property inspection before making your purchase is that you will be able to identify any potential issues you may encounter after your purchase. Investigations will point out if there is dry rot in sills, non-conforming wiring, or even mold. Some of these flaws may not be as dangerous when compared to others, but they can become more significant issues in the future.

When the home inspection reports list these issues, they are the means to negotiate a lower purchase price. Every problem found can be a cause for bargaining on the purchase price. If you discover that the property has flaws that need repair, you can bargain with the seller, who might agree to repair the defects or lower the home price. Besides, it will provide you a detailed report that is something of an "owner's manual" for the home. It will be a valuable document for the future in that it will include maintenance tips and schedules you should follow.

If the seller refuses to negotiate or make repairs, you have the legal right to walk away from the deal—and as long as you've placed some contingencies in your purchase agreement and you cancel your offer within the periods named in your contingency addendums, you won't have to forfeit your financial deposit.[1]

VERIFY ZONING

Visit the planning and zoning department at the local municipal hall. Verify the zoning that your property occupies; if you are in a single-family zone and you are purchasing a single-family home, then you are good to go. Zoning specifies how the land can be used. It also specifies the size and dimensions of the land area as well as the form and scale of buildings. It lists setback requirements. Does the property encroach on these setbacks? If so, it could mean difficulty in obtaining a building permit should you need one in the future.

About a duplex property, be sure to corroborate if it is legal or not. The municipal zoning department will tell you if it is a legal two-family home or a single-family that has been illegally converted. The issue with having more units than what zoning specifies is the building department could force you to remove a unit, or if the place ever had a fire and the insurance company found out it was an illegal two-family, they may not cover you.

However, verify if the property might be grandfathered in due to the building's age and it being non-conforming to that zoning area. If so, the municipality would have no issue with the property staying the way it is, and its owners would be welcome to repair or upgrade it. The only thing that may not be allowed is adding additional space or tearing the structure down and building another multifamily house on that lot. That is also true if it is fire damaged by more than fifty percent. That being the case, only a single-family home could be built to replace the fire-damaged structure to conform to current zoning.

A NON-CONFORMING STRUCTURE

A non-conforming use or structure is initially permitted, but no longer conforms to the specifications of the zoning area in which it is located.

FINANCIAL AND DOCUMENT DUE DILIGENCE

The purchase of an income-producing property requires the buyer to physically verify the existing tenant leases and examine each tenant's rental payment history. Verify the security deposits and, if needed, hold them in separate accounts if the landlord must pay and report the annual interest on the deposits.

A best practice is to analyze the seller's financial records and operating statements—assuming these can be obtained—to detect gaps in lease payments.[3]

Does the lease conform to the lease requirements where the property is located? Many small landlords simply download a generic lease from the Internet, not realizing that some of the conditions may clash with the state's tenant laws.

Check the lease for late fees charges. Do they exist? When are they due? How much are they? Do they exceed the tenant cap in that state?

Gather tenant names, telephone numbers, and emails so that you have them for administration purposes after you close on the property.

Another question to answer is whether the local municipality requires a certificate of occupancy for a tenant. If so, have the seller produce them.

Besides leases, there are other essential documents the buyer or his attorney will need to examine and verify. These include at a minimum the property's title, zoning regulations, property survey, tax assessment, and the seller's financial records and operating statements.

FULL DISCLOSURE

In most states throughout the country, sellers must disclose known defects to prospective buyers. This is often done on a form designed by the local board of realtors. Every community is different so there is no standard form. Usually, the form is exchanged on the signing of the contract, or sometimes it accompanies the listing itself. The disclosure form typically takes the form of a boilerplate document with a series of yes or no answers filled in by the seller to describe their home and their experience.

However, you should ask your real estate agent for a signed copy of the full disclosure form. The statement will be useful in aiding the home inspector to what specific areas he should focus on. As an example, if it is disclosed there has been termite remediation in the basement, make certain your inspector pays attention to it to make certain there are no more termites there.

NEW JERSEY ASSOCIATION OF REALTORS® STANDARD FORM OF
SELLER'S PROPERTY CONDITION DISCLOSURE STATEMENT

1 Property Address:
2
3
4
5 Seller:
6
7
8
9   The purpose of this Disclosure Statement is to disclose, to the best of Seller's knowledge, the condition of the Property, as of
10 the date set forth below. The Seller acknowledges that he/she is under an obligation to disclose any known material defects in the
11 Property even if not addressed in this printed form. Seller alone is the source of all information contained in this form. All
12 prospective buyers of the Property are cautioned to carefully inspect the Property and to carefully inspect the surrounding area for
13 any off-site conditions that may adversely affect the Property. Moreover, this Disclosure Statement is not intended to be a substitute
14 for prospective buyer's hiring of qualified experts to inspect the Property.
15
16   If your property consists of multiple units, systems and/or features, please provide complete answers on all such units,
17 systems and/or features even if the question is phrased in the singular, such as if a duplex has multiple furnaces, water heaters and
18 fireplaces.
19
20 **OCCUPANCY**
21 Yes   No   Unknown
22   ☐   1. Age of House, if known
23 ☐   ☐   2. Does the Seller currently occupy this property?
24   If not how long has it been since Seller occupied the property?
25   3. What year did the seller buy the property?
26 ☐   ☐   3a.Do you have in your possession the original or a copy of the deed evidencing your ownership of
27   the property? If "yes," please attach a copy of it to this form
28
29 **ROOF**
30 Yes   No   Unknown
31   ☐   4. Age of roof
32 ☐   ☐   5. Has roof been replaced or repaired since seller bought the property?
33 ☐   ☐   6. Are you aware of any roof leaks?
34   7. Explain any "yes" answers that you give in this section:
35
36
37 **ATTICS, BASEMENTS AND CRAWL SPACES** (Complete only if applicable)
38 Yes   No   Unknown
39 ☐   ☐   8. Does the property have one or more sump pumps?
40 ☐   ☐   8a. Are there any problems with the operation of any sump pump?
41 ☐   ☐   9. Are you aware of any water leakage, accumulation, or dampness within the basement or crawl
42   spaces or any other areas within any of the structures on the property?
43 ☐   ☐   9a. Are you aware of the presence of any mold or similar natural substance within the basement
44   or crawl spaces or any other areas within any of the structures on the property?
45 ☐   ☐   10. Are you aware of any repairs or other attempts to control any water or dampness problem
46   in the basement or crawlspace? If "yes" describe the location, nature and date of the repairs:
47
48
49 ☐   ☐   11. Are you aware of any cracks or bulges in the floor or foundation walls? If "yes", specify
50   location.
51 ☐   ☐   12. Are you aware of any restrictions on how the attic may be used as a result of the manner in
52   which the attic or roof was constructed?
53 ☐   ☐   13. Is the attic or house ventilated by: ☐ a whole house fan?   ☐ an attic fan?
54 ☐   ☐   13a. Are you aware of any problems with the operation of such a fan?
55   14. In what manner is access to the attic space provided? ☐ staircase   ☐ pull down stairs
56   ☐ crawl space with aid of ladder or other device ☐ other
57   15. Explain any "yes" answers that you give in this section:
58
59
60
61 **TERMITES/WOOD DESTROYING INSECTS, DRY ROT, PESTS**
62 Yes   No   Unknown
63 ☐   ☐   16. Are you aware of any termites/wood destroying insects, dry rot, pests affecting the property?
64 ☐   ☐   17. Are you aware of any damage to the property caused by termites/wood destroying insects,dry
65   rot, or pests?
66 ☐   ☐   18. If "yes," has work been performed to repair the damage?
67 ☐   ☐   19. Is your property currently under contract by a licensed pest control company? If "yes", state the
68   name and address of licensed pest control company:
69
70 ☐   ☐   20. Are you aware of any termite/pest control inspections or treatments for the property in the
71   past?

NJAR Form-140-5/04
Page 1 of 6

Figure 9. Sample Property Condition Disclosure Form.

Be on the alert for work that was done without a permit. When you visit the municipal building, you can ask to see the property's building permit file. Make a note of all permits and what they were for. When you visit the property, ask the seller about newer upgrades such as the kitchen, bathroom, added closets, and so on. You can then verify if a building permit was obtained as you have the file with you. If no permit was obtained, you may very well be responsible for bringing the property up to code if you should remodel. Unpermitted work needs investigation as it often means that wiring and plumbing do not meet code.

Buyers should receive property disclosure statements after their offer has been accepted, but this varies by area. A document known as a *residential disclosure form* is a statement prepared by a homeowner that lists and describes all known deficiencies in a residential property to a prospective buyer or a tenant. A residential seller's disclosure form or a home seller disclosure form must provide all relevant property information required by disclosure statutes.[4]

You want to ask for the disclosure statement as soon as the contract of sale is signed. In some areas, sellers provide the buyer with the disclosure statement before an offer is made. But whatever the case, it should be early enough to give buyers time to be aware of the issue before beginning the due diligence.

What Must Be Disclosed

The disclosure will consist of several forms, some of which are required by the federal government, for example, the existence of lead paint, asbestos, and environmental hazards. The documents are in the form of a checklist which specifies whether the home has or had issues such as the following:

- Windows and doors that stick or do not close
- Foundation issues
- Roof leak
- Problems with appliances or home systems like the HVAC
- All home repairs made on any of the above as well as insurance claims
- Renovations completed without a permit
- Pest or mold infestations

- Environmental hazards in the area (e.g., underground storage tank, floods, and wildfires)

ADA COMPLIANCE

Verify if the property requires compliance with the Americans with Disabilities Act. The ADA regulations vary from state to state. The federal government has created a checklist to help investors understand the rules before acquiring a building, property, or undeveloped land.

WHEN IS DUE DILIGENCE SCHEDULED?

The timing of due diligence can vary by location. But your real estate agent or your attorney can advise you on the details. On inspection day, you will have your first chance to thoroughly inspect the inside of the property that you are purchasing. It is most likely the last opportunity to review the property until the final walkthrough before the closing.

SCHEDULE THE HOME INSPECTIONS

Most lenders require a home inspection before you close on a purchase. There are two parties that the inspection report is written for, the buyer and the lender.

The inspection clause in a purchase and sale contract provides an agreed-upon time to conduct an inspection. Typically, it is ten days, though it could be different depending on what the parties agree.

The inspection is often three parts. It includes the examination of the physical condition of the property. It many states it will consist of a radon inspection. Radon testing is considered a specialty inspection. It is usually not performed by the home inspector. During a radon inspection, the inspector will set up special equipment to exam the basement to determine the existence of radon gas. Radon is a colorless, odorless radioactive gas that is produced by decaying uranium. Radon is present in nearly all soils and low radon gas levels are found in the air we breathe every day. When radon gas finds its way into your home and gets trapped, it can cause health issues. Lung cancer is caused by radon gas.

The third type of inspection is for termites and other pests that might be occupying the property. A home inspector often does report on an infestation. However, for best results, it is better to have a professional exterminator do the inspection.

These three inspections are paid for by the buyer, though they can be a bit pricey in some regions of the country, considering property insurance policies. You want to investigate what you are getting into in advance.

As a reminder, if your inspector finds something, the issue can often be used as a negotiating point to either repair the problem or change the purchase price. Your preference, however, should be a lower purchase price if the seller agrees to a repair under the circumstance that it may not be of the best quality if done correctly.

As a note of caution, an experienced home inspector can be an essential asset in the buying process. But they do not have X-ray vision. They will not be able to detect what they cannot see. They are not going to know if there is mold behind showers or inadequate electrical wiring in the kitchen unless lights flicker. So, understand that they will inspect what they can see.

Hiring a Home Inspector

For best results, contract a licensed professional home inspector to conduct the inspection. You can seek referrals from your real estate agent or your lender. However, easier still is the service offered by Zillow.com. They have a list of inspectors and reviews. It is called the Agent Finder tool and is helpful. After reviewing the inspectors' websites, you can seek a report sample to review and make your hiring choice.

Verify that your inspector is a member of one of these three professional organizations: The International Association of Certified Home Inspectors, the National Association of Home Inspectors, or the American Society of Home Inspectors.

The Home Inspector Agreement

The *home inspection agreement* (sometimes called a pre-inspection agreement) is the contract that you and the home inspectors will sign. The agreement is designed to protect the home inspector and the client from misunderstandings that may arise from the home inspection. It sets out what is and is not included in the price. It will list things such as whether testing for lead paint, asbestos floor or ceiling tiles and similar are included in the standard price.

The typical price charged for the average home inspection runs between $300 to $500 depending on the area of the country the property is in.

The Day of Inspection

Do not let the inspector do his work without you. Plan to be there alongside him, as you will learn a great deal in person. It is also probable the seller's real estate agent will be there as well, to answer the inspector's questions. The inspection should take a full half-day, so block off the time as you do not want to rush through this critical phase of due diligence. Do not join the inspector in the crawl space. They have protective clothing for that purpose. But follow along with him in all reasonably accessible places.

It will be an educational experience. The inspector will explain the home's systems to you, especially the heating and plumbing areas and the home's wiring. Also, he will give you valuable maintenance tips. Even though your inspection report will contain photos and descriptions, you cannot beat seeing it in person.

The purpose of a home inspection is to identify those areas that need attention. No property is ever perfect, even new homes. So be prepared to be disappointed at some of the findings. You are hiring an inspector just for that purpose.

The Inspection Checklist

During your introductory tour of the property, you should already be taking notes on what you want your inspector to pay attention to. An expert inspector will want to know your concerns before he begins his inspection. Use this checklist to help you focus on what to look for in your property tour.

Appliances. What are the ages and conditions of the appliances?

Attic. Is there enough insulation? How does the underside of the roof structure look? Are there stains on the underside showing old leaks?

Basement. A damp or wet basement is a sign that you will have mold issues. If not now, you will have them in the future if the problem is not abated. Mold issues can be serious. Mold can cause minor to moderate symptoms, but in some people, including infants and those with disorders affecting the immune system, exposure to even small amounts of mold can cause severe or even life-threatening health problems.[2]

Check for dampness. Look for sump pumps. Are they operating? Look for a French drain around the perimeter. If there is a crawlspace instead of a basement, let the professional inspector check that out.

Electrical. Are the switches working? Are the receptacles grounded? What is the size of the electrical panel? Is it updated? Is there room for extra appliances or a potential remodel?

Exterior. Check the outside condition. Is it missing shutters? Is there junk in the yard? Does the house look like it will need repairs or repainting soon? Are gutters and downspouts rigidly attached? Are there loose boards or dangling wires? Is there asbestos in the surface material, which would need added costs if it needed to be repaired or replaced?

Foundation. Properties settle over time, depending on the soil they are built upon and the type of foundation. Bring a golf ball, and if you are suspicious of excess settling, test it by placing the ball on the offending floor and see if it rolls by itself. On older properties, it is not unusual to find smaller foundation cracks. But a large crack could be a symptom of more severe issues. Inspect the base of the walls and the ceilings in each room. Are there cracks that might show signs of foundation issues? Look outside around the bottom of the foundation for encroaching tree roots that could be causing problems.

Heating and cooling system. Does it seem to do the job? How old is the furnace? If the system has been converted, are the old systems or tanks still in place? How old is the water heater?

Interior evidence of leaks. Check the corners of ceilings and especially around the windows in each room. If there is a fireplace, examine the interior for leaks.

Odors. Does the home smell? Can you detect what it might be and whether it could be fixed? Beware of musty odors that could signal a wet basement or sewer odors, which could signify old cast iron joints leaking.

Plumbing. Are the drain lines cast iron or galvanized, indicating that they are at the end of their life? Any unusual noises or malfunctions? Has the sewer line been scoped to check for potential cracks or tree roots?

Roof. What type of roof does it have? If asphalt, how many layers of shingles? What is its overall condition? When was it last replaced?

Yard. Check the yard for adequate drainage. Does the ground slope away or toward the structure? Are there any wet or soggy spots?

INSPECTIONS ARE NOT PERFECT

What if your inspection reports no issues and, despite a clean report, maintenance issues show themselves not long afterward? How does the inspection contract read? Inspectors cannot see through solid objects. They will miss hidden problems. However, if the problem was in plain sight that is altogether different. Does the contract allow for a fee refund, or will they pay for repairs? That is an unknown since we have no contract to look at.

SCHEDULE THE APPRAISAL

Your lender will want a property appraisal to corroborate its value. It is the lender who finds and engages the appraiser. As the buyer, you are kept out of this loop. You will be obligated to pay the appraiser's fee; the average cost of a home appraisal for a single-family home is between $300 and $425. In contrast, an appraisal for a multifamily building starts around $500.[5] Once the appraisal is complete, you and the lender will receive the report showing the value of the home. If the property's appraised value is reported at less than you paid, you might be able to negotiate a lower price or make a more significant down payment to offset a higher appraised cost.

HIRE AN ATTORNEY

When you have made your offer, you should have hired a real estate attorney. He will be invaluable in reviewing your purchase contract with you. Some states allow closing with just a title agency, and others will require the use of an attorney. Using an attorney who knows real estate law will help you overcome minor glitches in the purchase transaction. He will be an essential part of your buying team.

If you do not have an attorney in mind, your real estate broker can make a valuable referral to attorneys that are experienced in property buying.

PURCHASE HOMEOWNER'S INSURANCE

You will need proof of insurance for your lender before the mortgage is closed. Now is the time to find an insurance carrier to issue a homeowner's policy on your new property. The policy must be paid in advance. Many lenders will collect funds from you besides the mortgage interest and principal and the property taxes and pay the insurance themselves. They do not want the liability of allowing the coverage to lapse.

Check to see if you might need flood insurance. It is a costly policy if you do. You should shop around for your policy as insurance premiums can vary widely.

POST-INSPECTION

Many buyers and sellers think the real estate transaction is complete once the contract is signed. But that is not true. The negotiations only begin at the contract signing. Even in the most competitive markets, negotiations might continue once in escrow. That is because the inspection report often reveals issues that must be addressed, which may need fixing or a financial adjustment.

COMMON HOME INSPECTION PROBLEMS

Your approach to repair negotiations will depend on what is revealed in the inspection report. Your inspector will suggest repairs, both in person when you are with him and in more detail in his report. He will let you know what needs attention and what can wait. Listed here are the more common issues that come up in inspections:

- **Plumbing.** Leaking faucets, running toilets, low water pressure, slow draining, faulty water heater pressure release valve, drainage problems.
- **Mold and mildew.** Basements, bathroom, corners of windows, under the kitchen sink.
- **Improper grading.** Sump pump inoperable, basement dampness or standing water indicating that the home might be improperly graded, rain and other moisture sources that can seep into the property's foundation.
- **Faulty electric.** Receptacles lack grounding, no CGI receptacles in bathroom or kitchen, broken outlets, open junction boxes, circuit overloads.
- **Roof issues.** Curled or missing shingles and flashing, especially around chimneys.
- **Foundation issues.** Cracks, chips, slopes, other types of concrete degradations.
- **Appliance issues.** Improperly functioning kitchen appliances, smoke and/or carbon monoxide detectors, or other home appliances.

- **Heating and cooling issues.** Improper ventilation, improper heat distribution, dirty heating, or boiling systems.
- **Window and door issues.** Sticking windows and doors, cracks, draft leaks.

HOME INSPECTIONS FIND FAULTS

A home inspection of most properties will find issues. However, experience has shown that such problems are often minor and easily remedied. Such faults usually do not require extra negotiation. But if there are more important items that affect your decision to go forward, you want to discuss these with the seller. It is not the time for you to bring a lengthy list. The seller may just feel it insulting and refuse to accommodate you. You both can still back out; you if the maintenance issues are too excessive, and the seller because you are asking for a lower price. So be careful if you are thinking of negotiating.

The inspection report, and your real estate agent, can guide you in approaching these sensitive issues. Your real estate agent and your attorney can give you perspective on what may be reasonable.

For the most effective negotiating results, list what fixes are the most important to you, and ignore the minor ones. After you have come up with them, provide them to your agent, and he will pass them on to the seller.

Issue fixes before closing. It is common to ask the seller makes certain smaller repairs before the closing. You must consider that if the seller agrees to the fixes, they may not be of the highest quality as the seller's motivation is to save money.

Price compensation. It is best to receive a price compensation rather than need the seller to make a fix. It is valid for larger cost issues. If you find a serious drainage issue needing a French drain, as the new owner, you should hire and pay the contractor. For example, if you get several estimates for the work and present them to your seller with a request to take $12,000 off the purchase price so you can make repairs and eliminate mold problems, your seller might be convinced it is a fair price. If not, try to negotiate a price discount acceptable to you.

Barter for compensation. Bartering is a way to soften the sting of money requests when negotiating. You can ask the seller for items of value in place of lowering the price, such as a lawn tractor, appliances such as the washer and dryer, or the patio furniture set and similar. You want to make certain that they are items of value for you.

A Home Warranty. The smart idea is to ask the seller to purchase a home warranty to encompass the first year of ownership. It is especially helpful if the home has older appliances or heating and ventilating equipment. This warranty would include plumbing and electrical systems as well. If you think a home warranty can cover your concerns, it is worth requesting it from the seller.

INSPECTION NEGOTIATION CAVEATS

A post–home inspection negotiation is perhaps the most anxiety-ridden phase of the purchasing process. Both the seller and buyer are on edge as they do not want the sale to collapse. So, you must present yourself as willing to compromise. Yet you do not want to back down on issues discovered the seller should have known. But at the same time, if you wish to buy, you do not want to appear unreasonable.

Here are a few suggestions to help you ease the way in your negotiations with the seller:

Do not assume. Approach a negotiation with a positive attitude, but do not expect to achieve everything you want. It could happen, but it usually does not. Some sellers simply will be intransigent and stubborn. So, know in advance just what your dealbreakers are so if you cannot secure an important issue, you can walk away from the purchase contract.

Be a long-term buyer. If you plan on a kitchen renovation, then why try to negotiate over an old dishwasher or misaligned cabinet doors? If the home you are buying is older, then you cannot expect it to look bright and shiny. If it is something that you plan to replace in the future, such as a kitchen floor, then a broken or missing tile should be ignored.

Most inspections go smoothly, as do the post-inspection negotiations that follow. Use your agent's expertise to guide you through the process and keep your eye on the prize: owning your first rental investment!

THE FINAL WALKTHROUGH

The day before the closing or on the morning of, you will have the opportunity to conduct the final walkthrough. Make sure you take it. Make certain nothing is missing, everything is where it is supposed to be, and things are in the same condition you saw them in before.

What should be on your final walkthrough checklist:

- Bring all the essentials.
- Verify final repairs.
- Check for all items included in the sale.
- Open windows and doors.
- Carefully inspect the bathrooms.
- Review the condition of the kitchen.
- Test all the appliances.
- Try out the heating and air conditioning.
- Test the electrical system.
- Tour the property.

SUMMARY

Probably the most critical phase of the real estate investment buying process is due diligence. This phase begins once the purchase contract has been agreed upon and signed by the buyer and seller, though a purchaser often begins a preliminary pre-screening inspection before negotiations.

The due diligence procedure is time-consuming and tedious, requiring much running around. Because of this, formal due diligence is only conducted on properties that are under contract. The results of these inspections are concluded in various reports, including the home inspection, radon inspection, lead and asbestos inspection, termite inspection, and the appraisal.

Do not expect to negotiate every issue reported on these inspections. Instead, focus on structural issues rather than the aesthetic ones as no property will be in pristine condition, nor should you expect it to be.

As one of the foremost of the American founding fathers, Benjamin Franklin was fond of saying, "An ounce of prevention is worth a pound of cure." That is the purpose of the due diligence process: to catch the small issues before they grow to be costly repairs. The process will prevent you from purchasing a property that may succumb to expensive repairs in the future.

It is much more intelligent and financially favorable to walk away from a costly flaw now than to absorb the cost and find that you are running negative cash flow as a result. Such a circumstance may even lower a future sale price. Due diligence protects your investment, both now and for the future.

NEXT STEPS

Now that the inspections and documents have been reviewed, the next step is to coordinate a closing date with all the interested parties. This will include the buyer, his selling agent and attorney, your agent and attorney, the title company, and the lender.

The next chapter will help you understand the closing and what you can expect before you walk out as a new owner.

CHAPTER ELEVEN

CLOSING THE DEAL

"It is not a race to closing. This is about looking after the best interests of every touchpoint of a real estate transaction."
—Douglas Fish

The *closing* is the last step in buying and financing your investment. The closing, also called the *settlement*, is where you and all the other parties in a purchase and sale transaction sign the necessary documents.[1]
First-time closings can be anxiety-provoking and confusing for a new buyer. Yet, perhaps no closing can compare to the experience I witnessed while in Boston years back. A group of us were sitting in a conference room in the offices of well-known attorneys. The conference room was an attractive design in there were three conference rooms in a row. The walls between the conference rooms were glass. So, unless blinds were drawn, you could see from one room to another. On this occasion, the blinds were open, and we could see there was a group of people around another table in the next conference room. I was sitting on the opposite side of our table so I could see the activity in the other room every time I looked up. Soon I noticed that a few of the participants were becoming agitated and that even though the rooms were sound-proof, I could hear their muffled voices rising. It caught the attention of our startled group, who stared in disbelief as one individual stood up and hauled off and punched the well-dressed man seated next to him squarely in the nose.

That caused the rest of the people in the conference room to jump to their feet. One grabbed the man who threw the punch while others grabbed tissues to come to the rescue of the victim, who by now had a very bloody nose. A few moments of confusion followed, and then the group piled out, leaving an empty room with only a hint of what had happened from the blood-stained tissues on the table.

Red-faced, the law firm's attorney, who was sitting next to me, spoke up just as the door slammed shut," I apologize, folks. It was just one of those rough closings."

Concerned that this introduction might be a bit too brutal, I read it to my wife and asked her take." No, I have been to many closings with you, and nothing close has ever happened with us," she responded. "They were not complicated. All we did is sign documents."

"That is because we prepared in advance for the closing and reviewed the documents, so there were no surprises. I created a checklist for each closing to make certain we brought everything and knew who would be there," I reminded her.

I have never since attended a closing that ever came near the drama that one did. But there are times that a closing does not run as smoothly as I would have liked it to despite the best of plans. This chapter will explain the closing, what you can expect, and how to conduct yourself so your closing can settle without a hitch or a need for tissues. The more you know about your closing in advance, the more documents you can review before sitting down at the closing table, the quicker and smoother your closing will be. Still, there are always exceptions that can be caused by reasons beyond your control.

A successful closing needs careful planning of combining documents and people. But even with that, issues can crop up. As a result, agents and their clients suffer unnecessarily delayed closings and, sometimes, scuttled transactions.

THE TIME IT TAKES FOR A HOUSE CLOSING

A recent survey by the National Association of Realtors points out that closing on a house takes on average 41 days.[2] It goes on to report that one-third of all deals (32 percent) experienced closing delays. Forty-six percent were caused by "financing" issues. Twenty-one percent of closing delays were attributed to appraisal problems. Fourteen percent of delays and postponements arose from home inspections.[3]

The prime reason for financing fails is a dropping credit score in between loan approval and closing period. The lesson here is that a buyer must avoid buying on credit during this period. Hold off on significant items such as cars or expensive electronics or furniture until after the closing.

The second primary reason for mortgage failure is a shift in the buyer's debt-to-income ratio. It is often caused by the lender's discovery of previously undisclosed debts such as unreported child support payments.

WHY DON'T TRANSACTIONS CLOSE?

Credit challenges. It may surprise you that even though lenders have approved you for a mortgage, they continue to reverify your credit profile right up to the day of closing. They want to know if you are still employed, that you are not adding to your borrowing, and that you did not forget something vital on your mortgage application.

After all the time and effort put into a mortgage application, it can be heartbreaking to learn that a mortgage was denied at the last minute. The top reasons a mortgage is denied after pre-approval can be prevented. It is essential to understand why mortgages get denied after pre-approval, so you do not make these mistakes.

The main reason for such a denial is a drop in the buyer's credit score. Another quite common reason a mortgage is denied after a pre-approval is because a buyer takes on additional debt or a change in employment. If a bank discovers an adverse change in the income-to-debt ratio, such as court-ordered child payments that were not listed on the mortgage application, that could cause a mortgage commitment to be withdrawn. If your debt-to-income ratio changes for the worse, one of two things may happen: your loan will fall through, or your rate will change. Both of those things are wrong because your rate's only going to go up—never down.

TOP ⑨ REASONS
WHY CLOSINGS ARE DELAYED
IN REAL ESTATE

In the majority of cases, real estate closings happen on time as per the scheduled date. However, there are times when such closings may be delayed for any number of reasons.

01 APPRAISAL ISSUES.
If the bank appraisal comes in lower than the agreed-upon purchase price, this can easily delay or even nullify a deal completely if the buyer can't come up with the funds to close the gap.

03 INCOMPLETE AGREED-UPON REPAIRS
If the seller agreed to make certain repairs following an inspection and doesn't follow through on his promise in time, the closing date can come and go with no deal in sight.

02 MAJOR ISSUES ARE DISCOVERED AT THE HOME INSPECTION.
A home inspection is meant to uncover issues that will need to be either negotiated or repaired by the seller. If anything significant is revealed, the closing may be delayed until a settlement is reached.

04 INCORRECT LOAN DOCUMENTS.
When loan documents have inaccurate information on them, this can easily delay closing. It can be something as simple as the wrong contact information or as big as an incorrect loan amount.

05 TITLE ISSUES.
Last-minute title problems can creep up, including liens filed by unpaid contractors or the absence of a rightful owner on the purchase agreement, which will need to be rectified until the transaction can close.

06 BUYER FINANCING FALLS THROUGH.
The buyer may have been pre-approved for a mortgage, but it's not until an offer is accepted that the actual process begins. Many closings have been delayed or canceled completely because of failure for buyers to secure financing.

07 THE HOME CANNOT BE INSURED.
For whatever reason, it's possible for insurance providers to deny coverage for homes that have specific issues, such as knob and tube electrical wiring, which can increase risk and make the property uninsurable.

08 DISPARITIES BETWEEN THE GOOD FAITH ESTIMATE AND HUD-1 STATEMENT.
The Good Faith Estimate is what lenders must lawfully provide to buyers, and the HUD-1 statement is the actual line item expenses. If there are major disparities between the two, the deal will be either be delayed or won't go through at all.

09 PROBLEMS AT FINAL WALK-THROUGH.
The final walk-through gives buyersthe chance to make sure the home is still in the same condition as when they agreed to buy it. If something significantly different is noticed during the walk-through - such as missing or damaged items - a settlement will needto be reached before closing, which can

Figure 10. Reasons why transactions are delayed.

194

These are a few suggestions to help ensure your mortgage is not denied:

- Do not take on more lines of credit.
- Do not increase your debts.
- Avoid making large deposits into your bank without having proof of where they came from.
- Avoid withdrawing large amounts of money from your bank accounts.
- Keep up on saving money in case your closing expenses are more than first estimated.
- Provide all requested documentation to the lender in a timely fashion.

The terrifying walkthrough. The walkthrough is the prime reason for surprises on closing day, and for a good reason: this final inspection of the property takes place either the day before or the morning of the closing—so there is little time to prepare for whatever problems might pop up.

You might find that an overnight downpour flooded the basement, or appliances are missing, or you see settlement cracks that were previously hidden by furniture.

Money misunderstandings. On the day of closing, you must ensure that funds are available. You want to know if they should be transferred by a cashier's or certified check or wired. Often misunderstandings can have the funds land in the wrong account, and you can be left scrambling.

Title trouble. A title company—which confirms details about your property such as past ownership, liens, and the covenants—could bring up issues on closing day. Some problems, like tax liens or a claim on the property from a relative or co-owner, can postpone a real estate closing.

CLOSING PREPARATION

The first step to prepare for closing is to review a document known as the HUD-1 settlement statement. The law requires that you receive this information at least three days before the closing so you will have enough time to review. This document is at the heart of your closing as it lists your mortgage payments, the interest rate, and added fees that you will pay, called closing costs. As a guide, closing costs typically range from two to seven percent of your home's purchase price. The objective is to review and compare the numbers in this form against the good-faith estimate your lender provided you when they committed to the loan. Ask about any differences as discrepancies are not uncommon in the haste of putting documents together.

Thanks to new regulations in October 2015 known as TRID (which stands for TILA-RESPA Integrated Disclosure), you will receive your HUD-1 three days before closing so that you have plenty of time to check it over. (Before TRID, home buyers received this form only 24 hours ahead of time, which resulted in a lot of last-minute surprises and holdups.)[4]

CLOSING DOCUMENTS REQUIRED BY FEDERAL LAW

The Consumer Financial Protection Bureau provides a checklist of documents you can expect to receive before the closing that explains your rights and responsibilities and are used to record the transaction between the buyer and lender.

Loan estimate. This document lists important information about the loan. Traditionally, the lender sends you a loan estimate within three business days of receiving your application.

The closing disclosure. It lists all final terms of the loan. It includes all the closing costs, detailing who receives and who pays money during the closing. The closing disclosure is delivered at least three business days before closing.

The notice of the right to revoke. This notice tells you that you can turn down the loan three days after certain conditions are fulfilled by the lender.

The initial escrow statement. This schedule provides a list of charges the lender holds in monthly escrow, such as insurance premiums and real estate taxes.

Lender's obligation. You can cancel the loan for up to three years if the lender fails to give you copies of the 1) right to revoke, 2) accurate Truth-in-

Lending disclosures on the closing disclosure or 3) the final Truth-in-Lending disclosure.

Contractual Documents Include

A promissory note. It describes what you agree upon and provides the details of the loan. To include:

- How much you owe
- The interest rate
- When payments are made
- The amounts you will pay
- The length of the loan
- If and how the payment amounts can change
- The address where the payments should go

A mortgage or security instrument. It lists your rights and responsibilities as a borrower. It explains that if you fail to pay as you have agreed, the lender or servicer can foreclose on your home.

State and local government-mandated documents. There will be miscellaneous documents that fulfill state and local government requirements, generally to collect information and protect you.

Lender documents. Miscellaneous documents added by the lender, for example, an affidavit of occupancy.

Request that your lender provides all the documents in advance when you receive the closing disclosure. That way, you will have more time to review them all.

House Closing Checklist

The Consumer Financial Protection Bureau is a government agency that has published a helpful checklist designed to help a buyer's closing. You can go to its website and download the checklist.[5]

WHAT TO BRING TO CLOSING

You should make a checklist for your closing. Include all the items you will need to bring with you to the closing, so you will not forget any. These will include all your paperwork:

- Proof of homeowner's insurance
- Copy of your contract with the seller
- Your home inspection report
- Documents the bank requires for loan approval
- Government-issued photo ID

Your down payment: The HUD-1 form will specify your down payment and closing costs, so you will already know from your disclosure form exactly how much to bring. You will not be able to use a personal check. Ask in advance whether you should wire transfer those funds or if you will need to bring a cashier's check. You should also bring your checkbook to the closing, to handle any unanticipated cost that might appear.

WHAT TO EXPECT AT THE CLOSING

The closing team. Who will be at the closing and where is dependent upon the state you live in. But there are certain supporting people you can usually expect to make an appearance. Many states, mostly on the east coast, require the involvement of an attorney to close any real estate transaction, regardless of the purchase price, property type, or the parties involved.[5]

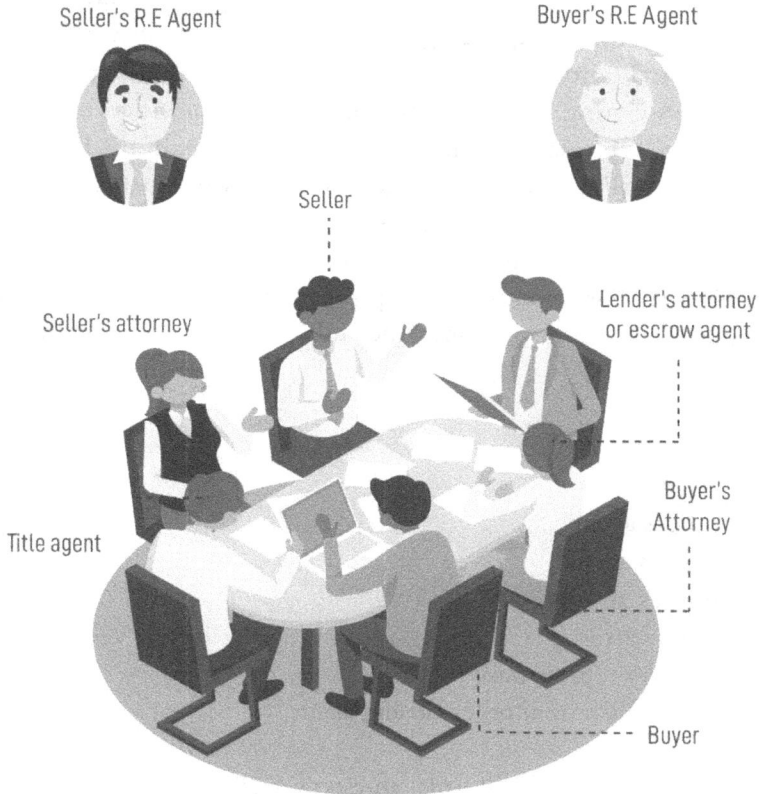

Figure 11. The attendees at the closing of title.

The escrow state. In states that use escrow companies, the company manages the transaction. The escrow company acts as the neutral third party directing the entire transaction.

The escrow company is a neutral third party, such as Chicago Title, that keeps the escrow account and independently oversees the escrow process, making sure all conditions of the sale are properly met.

The escrow company selects the vendors to outsource various parts of the closing process. This includes the document signing appointment, which is done by the notary loan signing agent. In escrow states, an escrow agent is used as the neutral third party.

With escrow closing, the closing is usually held in the offices of the escrow company. The title or escrow company is required to act in the best interests of the lender and will be the lender's agent. It is the seller that selects the title company. That is because the seller pays for the title insurance.

The buyer must attend the closing. If the buyer cannot be at the closing, he grants his legal representative with a power of attorney to act on his behalf.

Depending on local custom, the following people usually attend the closing:

- Buyer
- Seller
- Seller's agent
- Buyer's agent
- Buyer's attorney
- Seller's attorney
- Lender's representative
- Title officer or another closing agent

In a few states such as California, an escrow state, there may not be a traditional closing. The buyer and seller will provide instructions to the escrow company, then visit the escrow company individually to sign documents. The escrow company will conduct the closing itself without the buyer or seller, who are informed at its completion.

The attorney state. In an attorney state, it is the attorney that acts in place of the escrow company. The attorney directs the closing, acting as the neutral third party or representing the buyer or seller. The primary difference between the escrow company and the attorney closing is that much the closing is handled in-house by the attorney.

In attorney states, attorneys handle the loan document signing process in-house. And because of this, notary loan signings are not as prevalent in attorney states as they are in escrow states.

For attorney state closings, there may be as many as eight people present. That would include the buyer and seller, the attorneys for the buyer and seller, the title agent, and the bank attorney. Also, the real estate agents for the buyer and seller are often there to collect their commission.

TITLE SEARCH

Lenders want a title search before you can take the title to a home. It is a search of public property records to determine if liens or issues are preventing transferring the property into your name (which is rare, but if something does crop up. It's better to know that up-front).

Your lender will purchase a title insurance policy for its protection. Soon after the purchase contract is signed, the closing agent or your attorney will order a title policy.

The title insurance policy is a requirement before completing the closing on your new home. This policy will protect you and your lender in the unlikely event that your seller does not have a free and clear title. The purchase takes about two weeks to complete as different issues can affect that timeframe.

Expect to sign your name a lot. You will be putting your signature on a tall stack of legal documents (so be prepared for a mild hand cramp if you are not used to writing in cursive).

Signed documents are critical items for closing a property deal. You should read all of them yourself despite the ream of papers containing complex legal terms and jargon. It is essential to have your attorney explain any terms you do not understand.

It is normal to feel pressured by the parties around the table while they wait for you to sign documents. But take your time so you may read everything carefully. As they say, "Watch out for the fine print." Look for the interest rate to make sure it is what was agreed upon. Then look to see that there is no prepayment penalty. Make the last comparison to discover if original estimates favorably compare with the HUD-1 statement. Do not be afraid to speak up about any fees you did not previously agree upon. These have a habit of appearing, so look for them.

A few surprises. Though I assure you there will be no nose bleeds, be prepared for things to go awry at the closing; examples include someone getting there late, a document disappearing, or names being misspelled. All through the process, stay cool, calm, and collected as you will get more accomplished that way. Let your attorney do his work. Some closings can take longer than others. Just let it play out.

Now that It Is Over

After all, documents have been signed and checks have been exchanged, the property has been officially purchased. Your attorney or agent has the deed registered for you, which will be mailed to you later. You are officially the new owner of an investment property.

After the Closing

File your closing documents. You now have an enormous pile of papers that you need to keep safe for future reference. This means safely storing copies of all the paperwork that was signed during your transaction with the seller, from beginning to end. You will not be taking the deed home now, as it must be recorded. You will receive it by mail a week to ten days later.

Change the utilities. Hopefully, you have arranged with the sellers in advance to have the utilities switched to your name. If not, now is the time to call and make the change.

Change the locks. Changing the locks is always a good idea as you never know who has an extra set of keys. The lockbox key might have been duplicated, or the previous owners may have given a set out to cleaning people, a painter, a home stager, or similar service people. To be safe, you should change all locks now. That is why the first person you should call after getting the keys is a locksmith.

SUMMARY

As an investment property buyer, you will undoubtedly feel a great sense of relief on the closing day. After all, you have put in a great amount of work to get to the brink of your purchase. What you do not want to happen is to find the day is canceled or delayed due to a lack of preparation. Make certain you have prepared a checklist in advance, so you have not forgotten anything. Equally important, make sure you have reviewed and understand all the charges listed on your HUD-1 settlement statement. You also want to make certain on the final walkthrough the seller has fixed all the issues that you both agreed on and the property is in good order.

On closing day, make certain you bring all the closing documents you have previously been given, your government-furnished photo identification (driver's license or passport) as well as the funds to cover the real estate closing costs in the form of a certified or cashier's check. You will also want your checkbook to meet any unexpected payments if they come up.

At the closing location, expect many people to share the table with you; these would include your real estate closing attorney, the seller, the seller's attorney, the buyer, and the buyer's attorney. Also, expect to find agents of the title company and lender. Finally, be prepared to sign many legal documents before the property can subsequently be declared yours.

You will not need any tissues for your closing because if you followed our suggestions, your closing will go quickly and should be as smooth as silk.

Then congratulate yourself. YOU HAVE DONE IT IN THEORY!

NEXT STEPS

Now that you know how you can do it in real life. Use this book as your guide to your first real estate investment.

- Meet with real estate brokers that specialize in investment properties   (Week 1)
- Begin your search   (Week 2,3,4,5)
- Analyze properties   (Week 2,3,4,5,6)
- Make offers. The more you make, the more likely you will have an acceptance.   (Week 3,4,5,6)

- Negotiate a deal   (Week 4,5,6,7)
- Finalize a deal   (Week 8)
- Confirm financing   (Week 8)
- Schedule closing   (Week 9)
- Close   (Week 12)
- Celebrate   (Week 12)

Use the Investment Highway map on the next two pages to begin your journey to building wealth.

Once you start, you will build momentum and confidence. To help you stick to the 90 days, which is the title of the book, see the schedule next to the tasks and try to stick with it or better.

I wish you a successful journey!

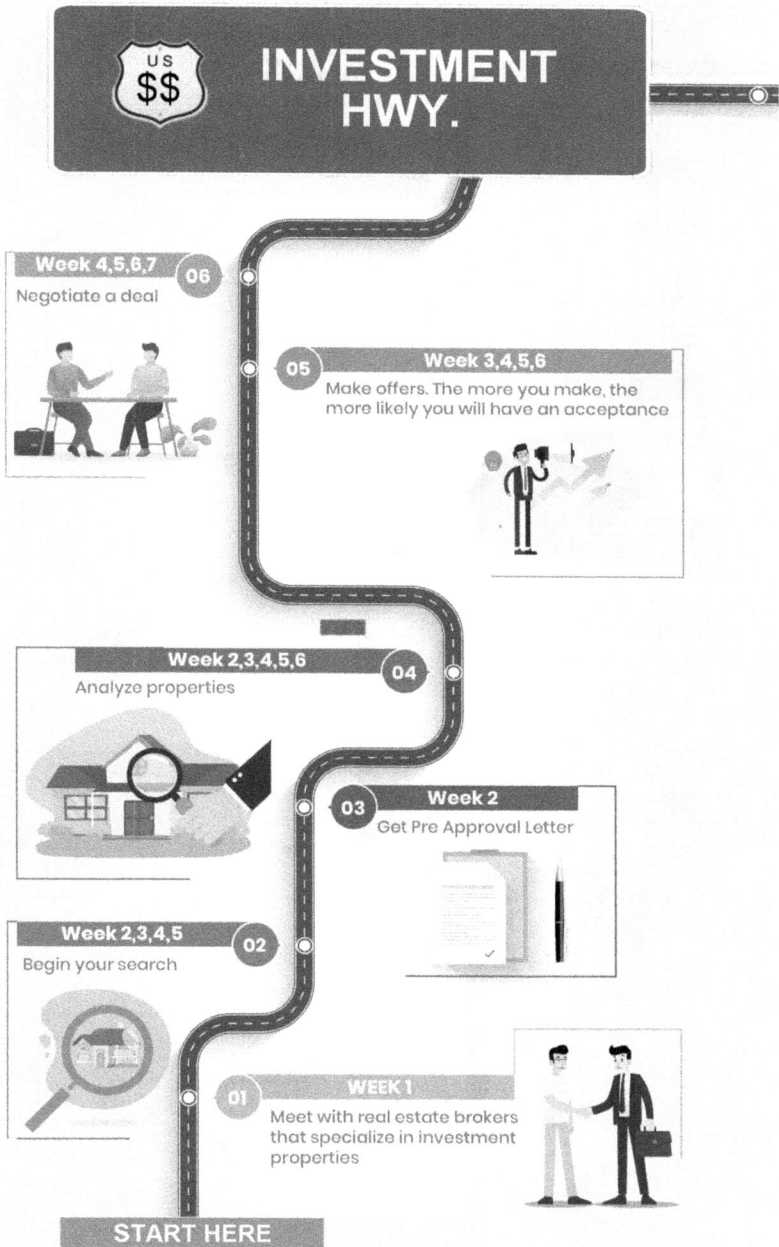

Figure 12. Traveling the investment highway to reach investment city!

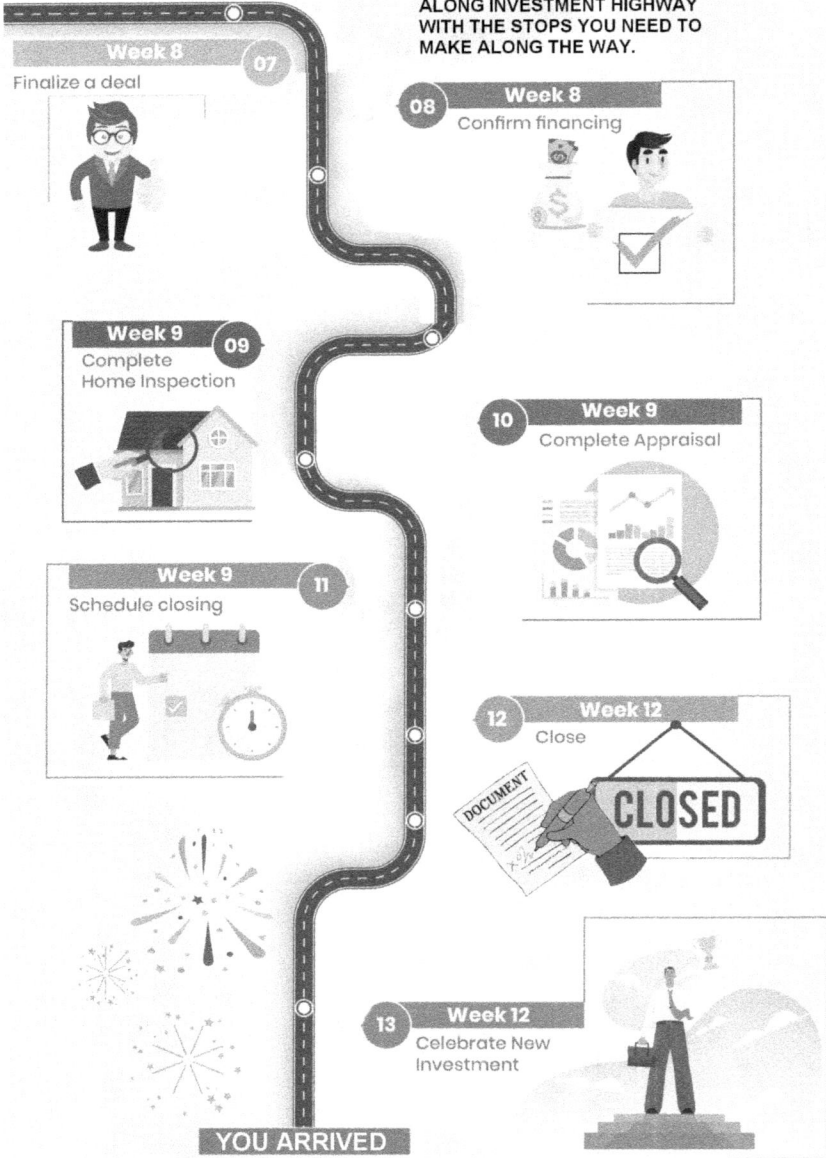

YOUR ROAD MAP TO SUCCESS ALONG INVESTMENT HIGHWAY WITH THE STOPS YOU NEED TO MAKE ALONG THE WAY.

Week 8 — 07
Finalize a deal

08 — **Week 8**
Confirm financing

Week 9 — 09
Complete Home Inspection

10 — **Week 9**
Complete Appraisal

Week 9 — 11
Schedule closing

12 — **Week 12**
Close

CLOSED

DOCUMENT

13 — **Week 12**
Celebrate New Investment

YOU ARRIVED

BIBLIOGRAPHY

CHAPTER 1

1) Bell, C., 2020. *Did You Miss the Stock Market Rally? You're Not Alone.* [online] Bankrate.com. Available at: <https://www.bankrate.com/investing/did-you-miss-the-stock-market-rally-youre-not-alone/>

2) Pavia, J., 2020. *Retirement Savings Last on Most Americans' To-Do Lists.* [online] CNBC. Available at: <https://www.cnbc.com/2015/04/09/retirement-savings-last-on-most-americans-to-do-lists.html>

3) Elkins, K., 2020. *Here's How Much Families Have in Retirement Savings—And How Much They Actually Need.* [online] CNBC. Available at: <https://www.cnbc.com/2018/04/23/how-much-us-families-have-in-retirement-savings-and-how-much-they-need.html>

4) Mae, S., 2017. *How America Pays for College.* [online] Salliemae.com. Available at: <https://www.salliemae.com/assets/Research/HAP/HowAmericaPaysforCollege2017.pdf, Page 6>

5) Mae, S., 2017. *How America Pays for College.* [online] Salliemae.com. Available at: <https://www.salliemae.com/assets/Research/HAP/HowAmericaPaysforCollege2017.pdf, Page 7>

6) LaMagna, M., 2020. *The Four Most Depressing Reasons Why Americans Are Not Saving Any Money.* [online] MarketWatch. Available at: <https://www.marketwatch.com/story/americans-are-more-confident-in-their-savings-for-the-first-time-in-six-years-2017-03-21>

7) DoItRight.2020.*MillennialInvestmentFears.*[online]Availableat:<https://www.ally.com/do-it-right/investing/millennial-investment-fears/>

8) Stinson, S., 2020. *Fear of Losing Money Can Set Investors Back.* [online] Bankrate. Available at: <https://www.bankrate.com/finance/investing/fear-losing-money-set-investors-back-1.aspx>

9) Maverick, J.B., 2020. *What Is the Average Annual Return for the S&P 500?* [online] Investopedia. Available at: <https://www.investopedia.com/ask/answers/042415/what-average-annual-return-sp-500.asp>

10) MONGABONG. 2020. *MONGABONG: "Never Depend on Single Income, Make Investment to Create A Second Source" - Warren Buffet.* [online] Available at: <http://www.mongabong.com/2015/07/never-depend-on-single-income-make.html>

11) Koppel, R., 2011. *Investing and The Irrational Mind.* New York: McGraw-Hill.

12) Vasishta, J., 2020. *10 Celebrities Who Are Also Superstar Real Estate Investors.* [online] DIRT. Available at: <https://www.dirt.com/more-dirt/real-estate-listings/celebrity-real-estate-investors-1203321201/>

13) Shpancer Ph D, N., 2020. *Overcoming Fear: The Only Way Out Is Through.* [online] Psychology Today. Available at: <https://www.psychologytoday.com/us/blog/insight-therapy/201009/overcoming-fear-the-only-way-out-is-through>

CHAPTER 2

1) Census Bureau QuickFacts. 2020. *U.S. Census Bureau Quickfacts: United States.* [online] Available at: <https://www.census.gov/quickfacts/fact/table/US/INC110218>

2) Horymski, C., 2020. *How Much Does the Average American Have in Savings?* [online] https://www.magnifymoney.com/. Available at: <https://www.magnifymoney.com/blog/news/average-american-savings/>

3) Frankel, M., 2020. *Real Estate Vs. Stocks: Which Has Better Historical Returns?* [online] Millionacres. Available at: <https://www.fool.com/millionacres/real-estate-investing/articles/real-estate-vs-stocks-which-has-better-historical-returns/>

4) Winzer, I., 2020. *Four Trends for Real Estate Investors In 2020.* [online] Forbes. Available at: <https://www.forbes.com/sites/ingowinzer/2020/12/31/four-trends-for-real-estate-investors-in-2020/#3981255c2797>

5) Trends, U., 2020. *Foreclosure Statistics & Trends | Realtytrac.* [online] Realtytrac.com. Available at: <https://www.realtytrac.com/statsandtrends/foreclosuretrends/>

6) Census.gov. 2020. *Median and Average Sales Prices of New Homes Sold in United States.* [online] Available at: <https://www.census.gov/const/uspriceann.pdf>

7) Millionacres. 2020. *Cost Segregation: What Real Estate Investors Need to Know.* [online] Available at: <https://www.fool.com/millionacres/taxes/depreciation/cost-segregation-what-real-estate-investors-need-know/>

8) Fishman, S., 2020. *How the Tax Cuts and Jobs Act Affects Landlords?* [online] www.nolo.com. Available at: <https://www.nolo.com/legal-encyclopedia/how-the-republican-tax-plan-affects-landlords.html>

9) Smith, L., 2020. *Leverage: Increasing Your Real Estate Net Worth.* [online] Investopedia. Available at: <https://www.investopedia.com/articles/mortgages-real-estate/10/increase-your-real-estate-net-worth.asp>

10) Corporation, F., 2020. *Fourth Quarter 2017, Volume 12, Number 1.* [online] Fraser.stlouisfed.org. Available at: <https://fraser.stlouisfed.org/title/fdic-quarterly-5153/fourth-quarter-2017-577883>

11) Trends, U., 2020. *U.S. Real Estate Market Trends – Realtytrac Real Estate.* [online] Realtytrac.com. Available at: <https://www.realtytrac.com/statsandtrends/markettrends/>

12) Corelogic.com. 2020. *Real Estate Solutions - Corelogic.* [online] Available at: <https://www.corelogic.com/industry/real-estate-solutions.aspx>

13) Cilluffo, A., 2020. *More U.S. Households Are Renting Than at Any Point In 50 Years.* [online] Pew Research Center. Available at: <https://www.pewresearch.org/fact-tank/2017/07/19/more-u-s-households-are-renting-than-at-any-point-in-50-years/>

14) Zillow Research. 2020. *Bold Predictions For 2020: Shrinking Homes and A More Stable Market - Zillow Research.* [online] Available at: <https://www.zillow.com/research/2020-predictions-26100/>

CHAPTER 3

1) The Real Deal New York. 2020. John Jacob Astor: The Making of a Hardnosed Speculator - The Real Deal. [online] Available at: <https://therealdeal.com/issues_articles/john-jacob-astor-the-making-of-a-hardnosed-speculator/>

2) Fadiman, C., 1985. The Little, Brown Book of Anecdotes. 1st ed. Boston: Little, Brown, p. 26.

3) Greene, D., 2020. Why Real Estate Builds Wealth More Consistently Than Other Asset Classes. [online] Forbes. Available at: <https://www.forbes.com/sites/davidgreene/2018/11/27/why-real-estate-builds-wealth-more-consistently-than-other-asset-classes/#753b15755405>

4) Fit Small Business. 2020. Best Turnkey Real Estate Companies 2019. [online] Available at: <https://fitsmallbusiness.com/best-turnkey-real-estate-companies/>

5) U.S. 2020. Real Estate Investors on U.S. Coasts Target Cheap, Out-Of-State Markets. [online] Available at: <https://www.reuters.com/article/us-usa-housing-investors-idUSKCN1271FL>

6) Buildium. 2020. Are Turnkey Rental Properties Worth the Risk? | Buildium. [online] Available at: <https://www.buildium.com/blog/turnkey-rental-properties/>

7) Michaelbluejay.com. 2020. Historical Real Estate Appreciation Rate in The United States. [online] Available at: <https://michaelbluejay.com/house/appreciation.html>

CHAPTER 4

1) Zillow Research. 2020. *Starbucks: Inspiring and Nurturing the Human Spirit... By Caffeinating Home Values - Zillow Research*. [online] Available at: <https://www.zillow.com/research/starbucks-home-value-appreciation-8912/>

2) Zillow Porchlight. 2020. *4 Surprising Things That May Increase How Much Your Home Is Worth*. [online] Available at: <https://www.zillow.com/blog/4-things-increase-home-value-224624/>

3) News, A., 2020. *The Walmart Effect on Home Prices: Economists Say Home Prices Have Increased Near Stores*. [online] ABC News. Available at: <https://abcnews.go.com/Business/economists-find-walmart-stores-increase-nearby-home-prices/story?id=16560451&page=2>

4) Business Insider. 2020. *11 Things That Will Trash Your Home's Value*. [online] Available at: <https://www.businessinsider.com/factors-lessen-home-value-2015-11>

5) Business Insider. 2020. *11 Things That Will Trash Your Home's Value*. [online] Available at: <https://www.businessinsider.com/factors-lessen-home-value-2015-11>

6) Business Insider. 2020. *11 Things That Will Trash Your Home's Value.* [online] Available at: <https://www.businessinsider.com/factors-lessen-home-value-2015-11

7) Pan, Y., 2020. *The Neighborhood Features That Drag Down Your Home Value—Ranked.* [online] Real Estate News and Advice | Realtor.com®. Available at: <https://www.realtor.com/news/trends/things-that-affect-your-property-value/>

8) Pan, Y., 2020. *The Neighborhood Features That Drag Down Your Home Value—Ranked.* [online] Real Estate News and Advice | Realtor.com®. Available at: <https://www.realtor.com/news/trends/things-that-affect-your-property-value/>

9) Pan, Y., 2020. *The Neighborhood Features That Drag Down Your Home Value—Ranked.* [online] Real Estate News and Advice | Realtor.com®. Available at: <https://www.realtor.com/news/trends/things-that-affect-your-property-value/>

10) Pan, Y., 2020. *The Neighborhood Features That Drag Down Your Home Value—Ranked.* [online] Real Estate News and Advice | Realtor.com®. Available at: <https://www.realtor.com/news/trends/things-that-affect-your-property-value/>

11) Trulia's Blog. 2020. *8 Features That Increase Property Values in My Neighborhood – Real Estate 101 – Trulia Blog.* [online] Available at: <https://www.trulia.com/blog/features-increase-property-values-in-my-neighborhood/>

12) Winzer, I., 2020. *Coronavirus Recession? What It Would Mean for Real Estate.* [online] Forbes. Available at: <https://www.forbes.com/sites/ingowinzer/2020/03/24/coronavirus-recession-what-it-would-mean-for-real-estate/#74cc15b52ad2>

CHAPTER 5

1) Wikipeda contributors. 2020. Multiple Listing Service. [online] Available at: <https://en.wikipedia.org/wiki/Multiple_listing_service>

2) Richardson, B., 2020. Nearly 40% Of Homes In The U.S. Are Free and Clear of A Mortgage. [online] Forbes. Available at: <https://www.forbes.com/sites/brendarichardson/2019/07/26/nearly-40-of-homes-in-the-us-are-free-and-clear-of-a-mortgage/#5ba4e12b47c2>

3) Connected Investors. 2020. Connected Investors. [online] Available at: <https://connectedinvestors.com/>

CHAPTER 6

1) Song, J., 2020. *Net Operating Income: What Is It? How Do You Calculate It?* [online] ValuePenguin. Available at: <https://www.valuepenguin.com/small-business/what-is-net-operating-income

2) The Balance Small Business. 2020. *Why Landlords Should Keep A Rent Roll for Their Property.* [online] Available at: <https://www.thebalancesmb.com/what-is-a-rent-roll-importance-and-key-terms-4691928>

3) Staff, M., 2020. *What Is Net Operating Income? | The Motley Fool.* [online] The Motley Fool. Available at: <https://www.fool.com/knowledge-center/what-is-net-operating-income.aspx>

4) FortuneBuilders. 2020. *What Is A Good Cap Rate & How to Calculate It | Fortunebuilders.* [online] Available at: <https://www.fortunebuilders.com/cap-rate/>

5) Rentalsoftware.com. 2020. *Real Estate Definitions: Debt Coverage Ratio (DCR).* [online] Available at: <https://www.rentalsoftware.com/debt-coverage-ratio-dcr/>

CHAPTER 7

1) Eplattenier, E., 2020. *17 Top Real Estate Negotiation Strategies from The Pros - The Close.* [online] The Close. Available at: <https://theclose.com/real-estate-negotiation/>

2) Listwithclever.com. 2020. *The Ultimate Guide to Lowball Offers: How to Make A Successful Offer.* [online] Available at: <https://listwithclever.com/real-estate-blog/lowball-offer/>

3) Evans, J., 2020. *Offering Over Asking Price on A Home: When to Pull Out The Cash And When To Hold Back.* [online] Real Estate News and Advice | Realtor.com®. Available at: <https://www.realtor.com/advice/buy/should-i-make-an-above-list-price-offer-on-a-home/>

CHAPTER 8

None

CHAPTER 9

1) Mortgage Daily, 2017. "3 Biggest Lenders Close over Half of U.S. Mortgages" [Press Release].

2) 2019. *2018 PROFILE OF HOME BUYERS AND SELLERS.* [ebook] National Association of REALTORS, p.8. Available at: <https://nationalmortgageprofessional.com/sites/default/files/NAR_HBS_2018_10_29_18.pdf>

3) Mortgage Daily. 2018. "Mortgage Daily 2017 Biggest Lender Ranking" [Press Release] Retrieved from https://globenewswire.com/news-release/2018/03/26/1453033/0/en/Mortgage-Daily-2017-Biggest-Lender-Ranking.html. http://www.mortgagedaily.com/PressRelease021511.asp?spcode=chronicle.

CHAPTER 10

1) Gordon, L., 2020. *What Is Real Estate Due Diligence? Find Out What to Do Before Buying a Home.* [online] Real Estate News and Advice | Realtor.com®. Available at: <https://www.realtor.com/advice/buy/what-is-due diligence/>

2) Mold-answers.com. 2020. *Mold Health Problems...Health Issues Caused by Mold Exposure.* [online] Available at: <https://www.mold-answers.com/mold-health-problems.html>

3) Kluwer, W., 2020. *Real Estate Transactions - Due Diligence | CT Corporation.* [online] Ct.wolterskluwer.com. Available at: <https://ct.wolterskluwer.com/resource-center/articles/due diligence-in-commercial-real-estate-transactions>

4) U.S. Legal Forms, I., 2020. *Online Real Estate Disclosure Form. Disclosure Forms | US Legal Forms.* [online] Uslegalforms.com.

5)   HomeGuide. 2020. *2020 Home Appraisal Costs | Average Cost of House Appraisal & Fees.* [online] Available at: <https://homeguide.com/costs/home-appraisal-cost>

6)   Trulia Guides. 2020. *A Final Walk Through Checklist for Homebuyers | Trulia.* [online] Available at: <https://www.trulia.com/guides/final-walk-through-checklist/>

Customer Reviews

★ ★ ★ ★ ★ 20

20 customer ratings

5 star		100%
4 star		0%
3 star		0%
2 star		0%
1 star		0%

Share your thoughts with other customers.

All reviewers ⌄

See all customer reviews ›

I would be incredibly thankful if you could take 60 seconds to write a brief review on Amazon, even if it's just a few sentences! Thank you -- Robert

>>Click here to leave a quick review

www.ingramcontent.com/pod-product-compliance
Lightning Source LLC
Chambersburg PA
CBHW071557210326
41597CB00019B/3281